MINI

SLOVENIA

How to download your Free eBook

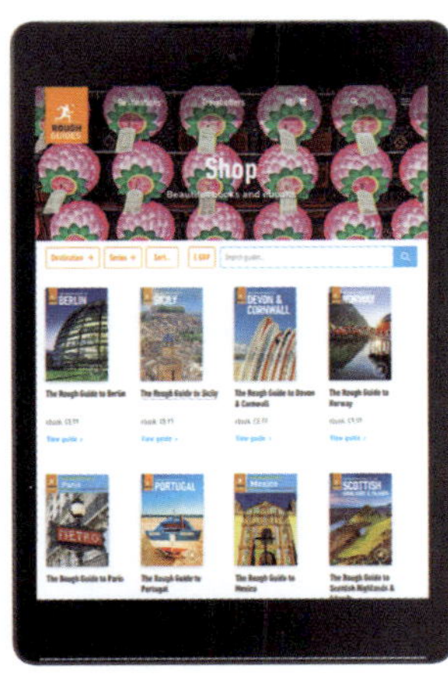

1. Visit **www.roughguides.com/free-ebook** or scan the **QR code** opposite

2. Enter the code **slovenia948**

3. Follow the simple step-by-step instructions

For troubleshooting contact: mail@roughguides.com

Samsonite

Contents

Introduction

Tiny Slovenia, no bigger than Wales, sits in Central Europe between Italy to the west, Austria to the north, Hungary to the east and Croatia to the southeast. With a 47km (29-mile) coastal strip lapped by a turquoise sea, snow-capped Alpine mountains rising more than 2500 metres (8200ft), tree-clad hills and fertile plains, it is gifted with an astounding diversity of natural landscapes. It is also culturally rich, tucked into a corner of the Adriatic Sea at the edge of both Western Europe and the Balkan Peninsula. But the country's greatest attractions are undoubtedly its dramatic scenery and unspoiled natural wonders, which make

WHAT'S NEW

Slovenia has plenty of cycling routes, but there's always room for more, and the 300km (186-mile) **Alpina Mediterranean Cycle Route** (https://bikeroute.si), launched in 2025, is an epic trail running from Italy to Croatia. More into rowing than biking? At Lake Bled, the new **Row with the Olympians** experience offers aspiring rowers the opportunity to learn the craft from Olympic athletes. In eastern Slovenia, the 106m (348ft) -high **Crystal Tower** (Stolp Kristal; https://www.stolp-kristal.si) took Rogaška Slatina's skyline to new heights, becoming the tallest building in the country when it opened in 2024. The glass-clad design takes architectural inspiration from the town's crystal industry; the views from the top are splendid. One for the oenophiles, wine producer Radgonske Gorice has launched **Untouched by Light**, a unique sparkling wine that's produced entirely in the dark, from grapes picked at night to wines matured underground in 168-year-old cellars and bottled in 99.8 percent black glass – the winemakers even wear night goggles. And Slovenia is easier to reach than ever: in 2025 Ljubljana was connected by train to Zagreb and Pula in Croatia for the first time in thirty years, offering travellers a more sustainable travel option.

Škocjan Caves, a huge hollow in the Karst mountains

a splendid playground for those who enjoy the outdoor life and adventure sports.

Natural playground

Slovenia knows how to capitalise on these assets, and visitors will find excellent leisure and sports facilities wherever they go. Almost half the country is cloaked in forest, while much of the remainder is given over to pastures, arable land, orchards and vineyards. The Alpine northwest is dominated by the tall, jagged mountains and peaceful green valleys of Triglav National Park in the Julian Alps, which is crisscrossed by a network of clearly signed hiking trails. Traditional, low-impact farming methods have meant that the remote peaks remain havens for wild animals such as brown bears, wolves, boar, deer, chamois and lynx.

WHEN TO GO

Slovenia has two main tourist seasons: summer (late May to early October), when it is warm enough to swim, and winter (from mid-December to late March), when it is possible to ski and snowboard. Accommodation costs skyrocket during these periods, and the cheaper places get booked up quickly, so if you're looking for a bargain you'll need to book in advance. Better deals are available in the shoulder seasons – spring and autumn – and these are also the best times for hiking, cycling and other outdoor sports, though bear in mind heavy rainfall is not uncommon as late as May and as early as September, which can put a stop to outdoor-centric plans. You may also consider timing your visit to coincide with some of the country's festivals: the Ljubljana Summer Festival brings the capital alive with musical performances in July or August, while over in Ptuj, the *Kurentovanje* (carnival) celebrations in February are utterly unique.

Winter snowfall in the mountains is substantial, and locals head for the well-equipped ski resorts with hire facilities and ski schools. In summer, the picturesque lakes of Bled and Bohinj offer the chance to swim in pristine water or rent a rowing boat. Close by, the River Soča is the place for watersports such as rafting, kayaking, canoeing and hydrospeed, as well as canyoning and trout fishing. There are also a number of well-maintained golf courses. For those with transport, the Slovenian Tourist Board has mapped several wine roads, leading through rural landscapes to vineyards and cellars that offer wine tasting and the chance to buy direct from producers.

Although Slovenia possesses only a small stretch of seaboard, the coast has been carefully developed, with three modern yachting marinas and a string of pleasant beaches, as well as high-class hotels and an abundance of seafood restaurants. Inland, the Karst region is contoured by dramatic limestone caves, clustered with stalagmites and stalactites, several of which are artificially lit and open to the public for guided tours.

In eastern Slovenia, which is flatter and more fertile, the principal attraction is the abundance of spas. The classic nineteenth-century Austro-Hungarian spa towns must now compete with twenty-first-century minimalist resorts that have thermal pools and wellness centres for pampering breaks. For closer contact with the country, visitors should consider the agrotourism centres scattered throughout Slovenia. These offer the chance to eat and sleep in a working farm environment.

Places and people

The largest city is the capital, Ljubljana, which has a population of around 300,000. There are no other large cities, but many towns have well-preserved historic centres, decent hotels and a friendly, relaxed atmosphere where life is lived outdoors in cafés and in authentic restaurants. Architecturally, the most interesting old towns are Ljubljana, Maribor and Ptuj, where the Baroque style predominates, and the coastal settlements of Koper and Piran, where buildings and monuments from the Venetian era are distinctive.

Lepena Valley – almost half the country is covered with forest

The population of the entire country stands at slightly over 2.1 million and is almost exclusively Slovenian. This is part of the reason the country had a relatively trouble-free divorce from Yugoslavia: with no substantial Serb minority to defend, Belgrade decided to let Slovenia go. There are, however, minority groups of Italians, predominantly along the coast, and Hungarians, mainly in Pomurje in the northeast, both of whom are guaranteed two seats in parliament. Slovenia's community of some seven thousand Roma is largely concentrated in the region of Pomurje.

During the Tito era, Slovenia received many thousands of economic migrants from the poorer republics of Yugoslavia, and with the war of the 1990s it also saw an influx of refugees. Some stayed and integrated into society, others returned to their homelands, and some remained in Slovenia but were never granted Slovenian nationality, leaving them stateless. The vast majority of Slovenes are Roman Catholics, while the Serbian Orthodox and Muslim faiths are represented in small numbers by migrants from the other countries of former Yugoslavia. There is a Serbian Orthodox church in Ljubljana, and in 2020 a mosque – described as one of Europe's most beautiful – finally opened, after much-thwarted initial plans and seven years of construction work.

The Cooperative Bank in Ljubljana, in Viennese Secessionist style

Historically, inland Slovenia, which was

SUSTAINABLE TRAVEL

Proactive government policies over the twenty-first century have made Slovenia a world leader in sustainable tourism – which makes it easier for visitors to lower their carbon footprint. Getting around is particularly eco-friendly: in Ljubljana, for example, public transport is either electric or runs on environmentally friendly methane gas, and if you're hiring a car you can use the Avant2Go electric-car sharing scheme (https://avant2go.si). Cycling is also a good option, with hundreds of kilometres of bike routes within the capital alone, and six designated Green Routes spanning the country. It's also worth looking out for businesses – hotels, campsites, restaurants, tour operators and so on – which have been awarded Slovenia Green certification, demonstrating that their services are designed with sustainability in mind. Explore the tourist office's top tips for eco-travel in Slovenia at www.slovenia.info/en/stories/choose-the-green-way-of-visiting-slovenia.

governed by the Habsburgs, used German as the official language, while the Venice-ruled coast spoke Italian. Still today, local dialects borrow from Italian near the sea, and German further inland. When travelling along the coast, you'll spot most towns and villages have two names, one Slovenian and one Italian, so that Koper is also known as Capodistria, and Portorož as Portorose.

Fluctuating fortunes

After joining the European Union (EU) in 2004, Slovenia experienced a surge in economic growth and optimism. By 2006 the national economy was flourishing, and in January 2007 Slovenia became the first of the new EU member countries to adopt the euro. Although the country suffered a financial downturn in the late 2000s and early 2010s – and again with the Covid-19 pandemic – it has successfully weathered these storms. Tourism, as a crucial cog in the wheel, has been instrumental in contributing to the country's prosperity.

10 Things not to miss

1

2

3

4

5

6

1. **LAKE BLED**
   A magical glacial lake in the northwest surrounded by rugged snowcapped mountains and forested slopes. See page 45.

2. **LIPICA STUD FARM**
   The home of the famous Lipizzaner horses. See page 60.

3. **PIRAN**
   Inspired by Venice, Piran is the loveliest town on the coast. See page 65.

4. **SOČA VALLEY**
   Pitted with rocky gorges, Soča Valley is a natural outdoor playground for intrepid types. See page 53.

5. **LJUBLJANA**
   The friendly, easy-going capital makes a good starting point for any tour. See page 33.

6. **POSTOJNA AND ŠKOCJAN CAVES**
   Duck underground to explore the subterranean marvels of the Karst region. See pages 59 and 60.

7. **WINE ROADS**
   Cellar visits and wine tastings are on offer in the vine-combed northeast. See page 78.

8. **KOPER OLD TOWN**
   The medieval quarter of Slovenia's main port is studded with beautiful buildings. See page 63.

9. **LAKE BOHINJ**
   Surrounded by the wild Triglav National Park, this is a great area for walking and adventure sports. See page 48.

10. **ROGAŠKA SLATINA**
    The country's oldest and most-visited spa town. See page 73.

A perfect day in Ljubljana

9AM

Early eats. For breakfast with a view over the River Ljubljanica, grab one of the outdoor tables at *Cacao* (Petkovškovo nabrežje 3; https://cacao.si), a few yards east of Prešeren Square.

10AM

City charms. Cross Triple Bridge (Tromostovje) and turn left along the riverbank. Visit the cathedral, Plečnik's Central Market (head downstairs for the fish market) and Dragon Bridge. From Krek Square, take the funicular railway up to the castle. Climb the Observation Tower for great city views.

1PM

Lunch. For something upmarket, the *Strelec* restaurant (https://www.restavracija-strelec.si) in the castle serves high-class Slovenian cuisine. For a popular local snack, try *burek* – a Bosnian-style pastry filled with cheese or meat – from a stall in the market (head for the southeast corner).

2PM

See the sights. Follow Ciril-Metodov trg past the cathedral and into medieval Old Ljubljana. Wander along as far as Upper Square, then cross Shoemaker's Bridge and pick your way to the charming French Revolution Square. Peek inside the Križanke Summer Theatre, then stroll up Vegova ulica, passing Baroque buildings and the National Library, to Congress Square.

3.30PM

Cake and art. Enjoy a Slovenian tradition by visiting the *Zvezda* cake shop in *Best Western Premier Hotel Slon* (Slovenska cesta 34). Order a coffee with whipped cream (*kava smetana*) to wash down your home-baked treat. Follow Cankarjeva ulica, passing the Opera House, to the National Gallery and the Museum of Modern Art, and pay a visit to both.

6PM

Evening stroll. In summer, take the underpass beneath the busy road and amble through Tivoli Park. Or return to the Ljubljanica and find a café for an early evening drink. In December, there's a Christmas market on the east side of the river, south of the Triple Bridge.

7.30PM

Dinner date. Linger over a relaxed riverside dinner at *Ljubljanski dvor* (see page 119) or *Ala Pršuterija* (see page 118). For a more stylish option in the old town, try *Julija* (see page 118).

10.30PM

On the town. Later, head for the cluster of bars strung along the east bank of the Ljubljanica, between Triple Bridge and Shoemaker's Bridge – *Captain's Cabin* (see page 101) is one of the best. For atmospheric alternative nightlife, head for Metelkova, a complex of clubs, bars and galleries in a disused army barracks (see page 102).

Outdoor Slovenia

8AM

Lake Bled. Day one of this action-packed outdoor adventure begins in Bled. Kick things off with a gentle amble around the iconic lake, then climb to the summit of Mala Osojnica for a perfect view or hire a rowing boat and paddle across the waters to the island. Finally, take in the majestic vistas from the castle, or if you fancy an adrenaline hit, soar above the trees on the Dolinka Zipline (https://zipline-dolinka.si).

12.30PM

Swim and lunch. Before grabbing lunch in one of Bled's excellent cafés, stop for a quick dip in the lake. There are plenty of swimming spots, and it's ideal for cooling you down after the morning's walk.

2PM

Vintgar Gorge. Just a short hop from Lake Bled is the Vintgar Gorge, one of Slovenia's most impressive natural features. Take the marked trail through this 250m (820ft) -deep limestone gully, to a soundtrack of rushing water from the river wending beneath you. The route ends at the beautiful Slap Šum waterfall; pause here for a photo stop, before making your way back to Bled on a pleasant trail through pine forest. See page 47.

8AM

Beautiful Bohinj. The following morning, take the road from Bled into Triglav National Park, heading for the banks of the serene Lake Bohinj. Hire a bike and spend the morning cycling the length of the southern shoreline, pausing at picturesque spots to cool off with a quick wild swim. See page 48.

NOON

Leisurely lunch. By midday, you'll likely have reached the hamlet of Ukanc (see page 48), where you'll be able to pick up a light lunch while you plan the afternoon's activity. Try the eponymous restaurant *Ukanc* (see page 120), an unassuming spot serving up delicious fresh trout to diners at outdoor tables on the summer terrace.

1.30PM

Alpine hike. After lunch, take the cable car up to the Vogel Ski Centre (see page 49), from which you can enjoy a walk high in the Julian Alps without the effort of climbing. Take in the splendid views over the lake and mountains before returning to ground level. Alternatively, if you prefer a more challenging hike, there are several walking trails beginning from Ukanc; the pick of the bunch is the route to the Savica Waterfall (see page 48).

7PM

Rest and recoup. Relax over a hearty dinner back in Bled and reflect on the weekend enjoying Slovenia's great outdoors – and begin planning your next trip…

Southwest sojourn

9AM

Postojna Cave. Away from the mountains of the north, some of Slovenia's finest sights can be seen on this one-day itinerary. Get an early start and head southwest from Ljubljana until you reach Postojna Cave (see page 59), beautiful limestone caverns that glisten with shiny stalagmites and stalactites in incredible formations (book a time slot to avoid disappointment). Don't miss the chance to see the remarkable "human fish" – an aquatic salamander so-called for its pale, fleshy colouration – in the adjoining Vivarium (see page 59).

11AM

Predjama Castle. Emerge from the gloomy underworld and head up the road to the splendid Predjama Castle, built into the rock of an immense limestone cliff. Wander the passages of the fortress and discover its history. See page 59.

1PM

Hrastovlje. After a spot of lunch back in Postojna, it's time for one of Slovenia's medieval masterpieces. In the tiny village of Hrastovlje, the Church of the Holy Trinity shelters outstanding frescoes depicting the *Danse Macabre* – one of the country's finest artistic treasures. Enjoy the audio tour and drink in every detail. See page 62.

2.30PM

Lipica. Next, it's onto the home to the famous Lipizzaner horses. At the Lipica Stud Farm you can watch these majestic creatures perform dressage most days at 3pm. The remarkable show is one of Slovenia's most unique experiences. See page 60.

4.30PM

Izola. After all that culture, it's time to relax. Head further southwest to the coastal town of Izola and linger over a coffee and cake in the pretty town square or on the seafront with views of the Adriatic. Izola is one of Slovenia's top beach resorts and on a summer's day, it's hard to resist taking a dip in the turquoise waters. See page 65.

6.30PM

Piran. The final stop on the tour of the southwest is the beautiful Venetian-style town of Piran. Wander the pastel-washed streets, embrace café culture in the town square, feast on delicious grilled fish and seafood at one of the town's excellent restaurants, then watch the sunset from the harbour. See page 65.

History

Slovenia may be a small country, but its history is remarkably complex. Perched on the edge of the Balkan Peninsula, through the centuries it has been repeatedly occupied, threatened and manipulated by outside forces, resulting in a proud national identity and a rich cultural repertoire.

Illyrians and Romans

The earliest known inhabitants of this region were called Illyrians by the Greeks. The most important archaeological find attributed to them is the fifth-century BC Vače situla, an ornately embossed bronze urn decorated with figures of men, women and animals, which was probably used for ritual drinking and is now on display in the National Museum in Ljubljana.

Roman ruins in Celje

In the first-century BC the Romans began advancing towards the region, and by the first-century AD they had conquered the Illyrian and Celtic tribes, and founded the inland garrison towns of Emona (Ljubljana), Poetovio (Ptuj) and Celeia (Celje). Developments within the Roman Empire were to have far-reaching repercussions for the Balkans: after the empire was split in AD 395, the fault line between the Western Church of Rome and the Eastern Church of Byzantium ran through the region. In the east the Orthodox sects emerged (Serbs, Montenegrins and Macedonians), while Christians in the west were Roman Catholics (Slovenes and Croats).

The Western Roman Empire collapsed in the mid-fifth century, and the region was stormed by Attila the Hun. The inhabitants of Emona, Poetovio and Celeia fled the Huns and founded Capris (Koper) and Piranum (Piran) on the Adriatic.

Early Slav states

The first Slav settlers arrived in the region during the sixth century, probably migrating from the Carpathian Basin. They occupied the river valleys, lived from farming and worshipped their own gods. In the seventh century they founded the Duchy of Karantania, the first Slavic state, with its centre close to Klagenfurt in present-day Austria. However, this was short-lived, as in 748 Karantania was swallowed up by the Frankish Empire (named Carinthia), converting to Christianity.

In 900 the Magyars invaded the region before being driven back by the Germans, who divided Slovenian lands among their nobility and the Church. Between the tenth and thirteenth centuries, monasteries sprang up across the landscape, as well as imposing castles designed to secure the borders against further attack.

The Habsburgs, Venice and the Ottoman Turks

The Habsburgs (whose family seat was originally in modern Switzerland) took control of inland Slovenia in 1335, splitting it into the Austrian crown lands of Carinthia, Carniola and Styria, and the royal family remained in power until 1918. During these six centuries, the upper classes were almost exclusively German, and the Slovenian language and culture was suppressed. In spite of the failure of repeated and determined revolts, the peasantry clung

FRANCE PREŠEREN

France Prešeren was born into a farming family in Vrba, near Lake Bled, in 1800. He studied law in Vienna then worked as a lawyer's assistant in Ljubljana. A vain and melancholy alcoholic and womaniser, Prešeren led a sad life full of disappointments. In 1835, following the death of a close friend, Matija Čop, and the realisation that his love for a local heiress, Julija Primič, would never be requited, he became suicidal.

From this time on, he wrote emotional romantic poems about unfulfilled love, the joys of drinking, and the beauty of his land and its women. He published only one volume of poetry, *Poezije*, in 1848, and his poems reached the public primarily through magazines. His work was unpopular with the Habsburgs due to its blatant anti-German sentiments, and was disapproved of by the Church, which considered his writing and lifestyle immoral. However, more than anyone else, he brought the idea of a Slovenian national identity to the people.

In 1846, he moved to Kranj where his house may be visited (see page 43). He died of cirrhosis of the liver on 8 February 1849, now celebrated as Prešeren Day, a national holiday.

on to their Slavic language and culture. Part of this was thanks to the Reformation: though the movement had little lasting effect on religion in the region, it did lead to books being published in Slovenian for the first time.

Habsburg power did not reach the coast, where towns came under the protection of the Republic of Venice, under which they remained until the Venice's dissolution in 1797. This accounts for the distinctly Italianate buildings, dialect and cuisine of the ports and fishing villages.

After 1453, when Byzantium fell to Mehmet II, both the Habsburgs and the Venetians became preoccupied by the Ottoman Turks, who advanced through the Balkans towards Central Europe. Entire towns were fortified, and many hilltop castles reconstructed in an attempt to protect Slovenia against attack. To fund such projects, hefty taxes were slapped on the local population, sparking further unrest and revolt.

The economic and social situation eased during the relative peace of the eighteenth century and the reforms under Empress Maria Theresa. Small industries were founded, and road links improved between Trieste and Vienna. Compulsory primary-school education (albeit in German) was introduced and serfdom abolished. This prosperous period was celebrated in the ornate Baroque style that characterises several Slovenian cities, notably Ljubljana.

The Illyrian provinces

In 1797 Napoleon conquered the Venetian Empire and a dozen years later succeeded in cutting Vienna off from the coast by taking Slovenia into his so-called Illyrian Provinces, stretching from Graz in Austria all the way down the Eastern Adriatic to include Dalmatia.

Napoleon found favour among the Slovenes by making Ljubljana the capital of the Illyrian Provinces, and by allowing them to use Slovenian, rather than German, as the official language in schools and administration. This period of French rule also gave birth to

Ancient stone wall with detail showing the Lion of St Mark, the symbol of Venice

the dream of a southern Slav state, which would unite Croats, Serbs and Slovenes, all of whom were represented in the Illyrian Provinces. But when Napoleon's defeat in Russia in 1813 presaged the end of his empire two years later, Slovenia fell once again to Vienna.

Dreams of independence

Once back in power, the Habsburgs set about suppressing Slovenian national aspirations and reinstalling the feudal system. But Slovenian pride and the dream of independence had taken root. It became the theme of the romantic poet France Prešeren (1800–49), author of *Zdravljica* (*A Toast*, 1844), which was chosen as the Slovenian national anthem when the country finally gained full independence in 1991. In 1848 Slovenian intellectuals founded the Zedinjena Slovenija (United Slovenia) movement, whose aim was to unify the Slovenian people and gain recognition of the Slovenian language. It did not succeed, but it inspired later movements.

A metal disc marks the border between Italy and Slovenia in Transalpine Square

Meanwhile, railways were arriving and industrialisation was taking place. Vienna was linked to Maribor in 1846, and a line extended through Ljubljana to Trieste in 1857.

World wars and the Kingdom of Yugoslavia

Statue of the national poet France Prešeren in Ljubljana

When the Habsburg Archduke Franz Ferdinand was assassinated by a Serb nationalist in Sarajevo in 1914, World War I broke out. Italy entered the conflict on the side of Britain, France and Russia, having been promised a portion of Slovenian territory as a reward. The result: bloody fighting along the River Soča (Isonzo in Italian), or the Isonzo Front (see page 52). Slovenes had the impossible choice of siding with the Habsburgs to keep their country intact, or opposing them and fighting fellow Slavs.

The defeat of the Austro-German alliance in 1918 saw the end of the Habsburg Empire. Inland Slovenia became part of the newly formed Kingdom of Serbs, Croats and Slovenes (in 1929 renamed the Kingdom of Yugoslavia, meaning Land of Southern Slavs) under Peter I, while the Slovenian coast, as promised, was handed to Italy.

In 1941, Hitler declared war on the Kingdom of Yugoslavia. King Peter II deserted Belgrade for London, and the country was occupied by Axis forces, with Slovenia partitioned between Germany, Hungary and Italy. Josip Broz Tito, half-Slovene, half-Croat by birth and leader of the Yugoslav Communist Party, set up the anti-fascist Partizan (Partisan) resistance movement, which succeeded in liberating the country in 1945.

With the war over and the monarchy gone, the Kingdom of Yugoslavia became the Socialist Federal Republic of Yugoslavia, made up of six republics including Slovenia, with Tito as President. Thousands of Slovenian and Croatian Nazi collaborators fled over the border to Austria, but British forces caught them in Bleiburg, disarmed them and sent them back to Yugoslavia, where many were executed.

Tito turned Yugoslavia into an extraordinary country. In 1948 he broke with the USSR, but he remained on amicable terms with both the communist East and capitalist West, gaining favours from both. Unlike the strict communism practised in the countries of the Eastern Bloc, Yugoslavian communism consisted of a market economy based on workers' self-management (cooperatives), and citizens were free to travel abroad, while foreigners could enter the country without visas. During the 1960s, the economy flourished, thanks to increased industrialisation and the beginnings of organised tourism. However, the gap between the richer and poorer republics also grew, and the tourist coastal areas of Slovenia and Croatia objected to subsidising the poorer regions.

It was only Tito's remarkable charisma, and his belief in *Bratstvo i Jedinstvo* (Brotherhood and Unity) that held Yugoslavia together and kept nationalist aspirations at bay. Before his death in 1980, after 35 years in power, he attempted to prevent any one republic becoming too dominant by establishing a rotating presidency, so that each republic should take the helm for one year. But it was not to work.

Opposition and independence

During the 1980s, Slovenia found itself producing 25 percent of Yugoslavia's export goods, despite making up only eight percent of the population. With profits being siphoned by Belgrade, the Slovenes grew increasingly frustrated. In 1988, the Yugoslavian People's Army (JNA) Military Council arrested and put on trial three journalists working for *Mladina*, a weekly satirical magazine. This triggered further disenchantment and dissent and, soon after, the creation of an organised Slovenian opposition movement, precipitating Slovenia's eventual secession from Yugoslavia.

Partisans on the entrance to the Parliament Building

Meanwhile, in Serbia, Slobodan Milošević was fomenting a new wave of Serbian nationalism. In 1988, following riots by ethnic Albanians in Kosovo, he clamped down on the province by stripping it of autonomy. This exhibition of power bode ill for tiny Slovenia, but the international community showed very little interest. With the fall of the Berlin Wall in 1989 marking the end of Eastern Bloc communism, Yugoslavia was no longer important to Western strategic interests.

Slovenia's first show of defiance against Belgrade arose in January 1990, when Slovenian delegates, angered by Serbian and Montenegrin rejection of all of their proposals, walked out of the 14th Congress of the Yugoslav Communist Party. In April, Slovenia held multiparty elections and a non-communist government was formed, bringing with it calls for autonomy. Slovenia staged a referendum in December, in which 88 percent of the electorate voted for independence. Belgrade rejected Slovenia's request for secession.

NOTES

In 1992 the names of 18,000 people who had been living in Slovenia without acquiring citizenship were removed from the registry of residents, losing their right to work, health and education. Known as "The Erased", their story is explored in a 2018 Slovenian film of the same name.

Nevertheless, Slovenia declared independence on 25 June 1991, the same day as neighbouring Croatia, where Serbs formed a substantial minority. The following day, the JNA began moving towards the border, where it was met by Slovenian territorial defence units that had been stockpiling and importing arms. After a conflict known as the 'Ten-Day War', in which around 75 people died, Milošević had a change of mind and the JNA retreated into Croatia. Independence was assured, and in May 1992 Slovenia was admitted to the United Nations.

Modern Slovenia

Following independence, the country's economy initially slid into decline, as Slovenia had lost its natural trading partners – the other former Yugoslav republics, several of which were at war – and gained an influx of refugees. Nevertheless, the country managed to return to prosperity, and the electorate strongly endorsed the centre-left government's application to join the European Union with an 89.6 percent 'yes' vote in a 2003 referendum. Membership meant an injection of funds and, by 2004, the economy picked up so much that when Slovenia entered the EU on 1 May it had the healthiest financial status of all ten new members.

Slovenia was the first new member country to fulfil the EU's Maastricht criteria for inflation and adopted the euro on 1 January 2007. It was also the inaugural new member state to hold the Presidency of the Council of the European Union in 2008, a role which it reclaimed in 2021.

The country was greatly affected by the global economic slowdown of 2008, and its financial crisis deepened over the next five years, before recovering yet again over the following decade. Politically, the early 2010s saw several governments come and go, as well as mass anti-establishment protests in late 2012; stability returned in the middle of the decade, though in 2018 the ruling government was toppled following a referendum on the construction of a new railway line between Ljubljana and Koper.

The outbreak of the Covid-19 pandemic sparked a similar crisis-management strategy in line with most European nations. By 2022, all lockdown measures were repealed, and that year also saw the election of the centre-left Freedom Movement party, under Robert

Slovenian government building

Golob, to parliament. In 2025, simmering discontent on defence spending led Golob to announce an upcoming referendum on whether Slovenia should remain in NATO – the Parliament later overturned the decision for a vote.

Chronology

1st century BC Romans arrive.

6th century AD Slav settlers arrive.

8th century Region comes under Frankish domination. Slovenes convert to Christianity.

9th century Region passes to Dukes of Bavaria.

13th century Coastal towns take Venetian protectorate.

1335 Habsburgs take inland Slovenia.

15th and 16th centuries Ottoman Turks advance into the Balkans. Hilltop castles are built for defence. Succession of peasant uprisings.

1797 Fall of Venetian Empire. Coastal towns pass to Habsburgs.

1809 Slovenia absorbed into Napoleon's Illyrian Provinces.

1814 Fall of Napoleon. Slovenia back under Habsburg control.

1918 Fall of Austro-Hungary. Inland Slovenia becomes part of Kingdom of Serbs, Croats and Slovenes. Coast passes to Italy.

1941 Hitler declares war on Yugoslavia. Slovenia occupied by Axis forces.

1945 Tito founds Socialist Federal Republic of Yugoslavia, with Slovenia as one of six constituent republics.

1980 Tito dies, leaving Yugoslavia with rotating presidency.

1980s Economic crisis. Slovenia and Croatia object to funding poorer republics. Milošević in power in Belgrade as Serbian nationalism grows.

1989 Fall of Berlin Wall marks breakdown of Eastern Bloc and demise of communist ideals in Europe.

1990 Non-communist government elected.

1991 Slovenia proclaims independence. 'Ten-Day War' ensues.

1992 EU and UN recognise Slovenia.
2004 Slovenia joins EU along with nine other countries.
2007 Slovenia adopts the euro.
2017 An international court of arbitration rules that Slovenia has the right to use a corridor crossing Croatian waters in the Adriatic.
2020 Covid-19 pandemic leads to lockdown throughout Slovenia.
2022 Freedom Movement's Robert Golob becomes prime minister.
2022 Same-sex marriage legalised after a Constitutional Court ruling.
2023 In August, floods in northern, central and eastern Slovenia are considered the worst natural disaster in the country's modern history.
2025 Slovenia's parliament overturns the government's decision to hold a referendum on NATO membership.

Golob at the Third European Political Community Summit

A beautiful view of Ljubljana

Places

Slovenia is small, compact and incredibly diverse. From the central location of Ljubljana, almost anywhere can be reached within two hours. If you don't have a car, efficient buses link the capital to the most remote regions.

First-time visitors should start in Ljubljana, then venture to the sublime mountains and lakes of the northwest and round off with the splendid Venetian coastal towns in the southwest. The main draws of the northwest are the majestic alpine landscape of Triglav National Park and the turquoise River Soča. The southwest is known for its 'coast and karst': the Italianate sea towns of Koper and Piran, the commercial resort of Portorož, plus the mysterious caves of Postojna and Škocjan, and Lipica Stud Farm. Less visited by foreigners but dear to many Slovenes, the southeast's architectural treasures include the monasteries and castles of Krka Valley, plus several spas. The flatter landscape of the northeast leads to the border with Hungary and the old Baroque towns of Maribor, Ptuj and Celje; there are also sophisticated thermal spas and a network of wine roads with cellars open to the public.

Ljubljana

Highlights

- **Around Prešeren Square**, see page 35
- **The old town**, see page 36
- **The castle**, see page 38
- **The centre**, see page 38
- **Tivoli Park and beyond**, see page 40

Compact and friendly, **Ljubljana** ❶ is a remarkably easy-going city. The River Ljubljanica, crossed by elegant bridges and lined with weeping willows and open-air cafés, flows through the heart

The rose-red Franciscan Church by the River Ljubljanica

of the old town, lending a relaxed air to the cobbled streets and Baroque buildings, with the whole ensemble presided over by a proud hilltop castle. The city was founded in the first century BC by the Romans, who built a fortified military encampment named Emona, on the left bank of the river, which was destroyed by the Huns in the mid-fifth-century AD. Slavs founded a second settlement on the right bank below the castle hill in the area that is now Old Square (Stari trg) and Town Square (Mestni trg), the heart of the city in the Middle Ages. This was largely ravaged by an earthquake in 1511 and rebuilt in Baroque style. After another earthquake, in 1895, new buildings were constructed in the Secessionist style – often referred to as the Viennese Art Nouveau.

In the 1980s, Ljubljana was Yugoslavia's centre of underground culture, with punk rock bands and satirical magazines. Today, the alternative scene lives on through the thriving student community, a large chunk of the city's 300,000-strong population.

Around Prešeren Square

Lying at the heart of the city is **Prešeren Square** (Prešernov trg), giving onto the Ljubljanica. Watched over by a bronze statue of poet France Prešeren (1800–49; see page 22), this square has a couple of notable Secessionist buildings: the **Palača Urbanc**, occupied by Galerija Emporium, Ljubljana's oldest department store, and the **Hauptman House** (Hauptmanova hiša). To the left of the latter is a small relief of Julija, Prešeren's lifelong love. City-dwellers meet on the steps that lead up the rose-and-cream facade of the seventeenth-century Baroque **Franciscan Church** (Frančiškanska cerkev).

Miklošičeva, the thoroughfare to the right of the church, is peppered with Secessionist buildings, notably the white **Grand Hotel Union** by Josip Vancaš (1905) and the elegant former Cooperative Bank by Ivan and Helena Vurnik (1922), with colourful geometric patterns. Miklošičeva leads north to the train and bus stations.

JOŽE PLEČNIK

Born in Ljubljana in 1872, Plečnik studied architecture in Vienna under the great early Modernist Otto Wagner, moving in 1911 to Prague where he supervised the renovation of Hradčany Castle and lectured at the School of Arts and Crafts. He returned to Ljubljana in 1921, became head of the university's new Faculty of Architecture, and set about transforming the face of the city, adding the Triple Bridge, the Shoemaker's Bridge, the National and University Library, Križanke Summer Theatre, Trnovo Bridge, the Central Market, Žale Cemetery and the Church of St Michael on the Marshes, all in a curious blend of Classical and Art Deco. **Plečnik House** (Plečnikova hiša), his charming former home and studio, is at Karunova 4–6, in the eastern suburb of Trnovo (charge; https://mgml.si/en/plecnik-house).

Dragon Bridge – the dragons are said to wag their tails

From Prešeren Square the splendid white, three-span **Triple Bridge** Ⓐ (Tromostovje) by Jože Plečnik connects the city centre to the old town and gives visitors their first taste of the ingenious works of the famous architect.

Just across the Triple Bridge is the **Slovenian Tourist Information Centre** (tel: 01-306 12 15; www.visitljubljana.com), where you can buy the Ljubljana card for entry to most of the city's museums, as well as book places on guided city tours, collect free brochures and maps, or hire bikes.

The old town

Though largely Baroque, the old town dates back to medieval times and is the only part of the city to have survived the 1895 earthquake. To the right of the Triple Bridge, the waterside promenade of **Cankarjevo nabrežje** is packed with cafés and holds the Sunday morning **flea market**, where stalls are piled with antiques and bric-a-brac, including memorabilia of Communist Yugoslavia.

Left of the Triple Bridge lies the **Central Market** (Glavna tržnica), an open-sided colonnade designed by Plečnik in 1939. It runs upstream all the way to the Art Nouveau **Dragon Bridge** (Zmajski most). Inside the Central Market, the lower level beside the water has fishmongers' stalls, while the upper level accommodates a variety of goods. The landward side opens onto **Vodnik Square** (Vodnikov trg), where a colourful market is held on weekdays and Saturday mornings, with stallholders selling seasonal fruit and vegetables, fresh flowers, honey, beeswax candles, dried herbs and clothes.

West of Vodnik Square stands the eighteenth-century Baroque **Cathedral of St Nicholas** (Stolna cerkev svetega Nikolaja), the work of by Italian architect and Jesuit monk Andrea Pozzo. Close to the river, it is aptly dedicated to St Nicholas, the protector of sailors and fishermen. The modern bronze doors commemorate Pope John Paul II's visit in 1996.

Close by is **Town Square** (Mestni trg), a cobbled square overlooked by the eighteenth-century **Town Hall** (Rotovž). The

WHERE TO SHOOT THE BEST PHOTOGRAPHS

The Triple Bridge, Ljubljana From just outside Ljubljana's tourist office, you can take a lovely picture of the Triple Bridge and the Franciscan church in the background. Come before midday for the best light on the church. See page 36.

Mala Osojnica, Bled The classic photo of Lake Bled, with the island and church in the foreground and the castle and mountains behind, is best taken from the viewpoint of Mala Osojnica. A sunny evening is the ideal time. See page 45.

Predjama Castle, Predjama One of Europe's most impressive castles, Predjama is built into a rock face. A convenient viewpoint has been built opposite, affording the best angle for photos. See page 59.

Town walls, Piran Piran is a photogenic place from pretty much any angle, but perhaps the top shot can be found on the medieval walls. From here, you can look down on the Venetian-style church tower, perfectly framed against the blue Adriatic. See page 65.

Mount Triglav If you've sweated your way up to the summit of Slovenia's highest mountain, you'll want a photo to remember it by. Fortunately, the surrounds are gorgeous: point the camera in any direction and you'll capture splendid mountain vistas. See page 93.

charming Baroque **Robba Fountain** (Robbov vodnjak), a three-sided obelisk, was designed by the Italian Francesco Robba in 1751 to represent Slovenia's three rivers, the Ljubljanica, Sava and Krka. Town Square leads to **Old Square** Ⓑ (Stari trg), with elegant pastel-coloured Baroque buildings housing lively cafés, boutiques and galleries, and becomes **Upper Square** (Gornji trg).

The castle

A signed path to the left of Upper Square cuts through woodland to the top of the castle hill, which is crowned by **Ljubljana Castle** Ⓒ (Ljubljanski grad; charge; www.ljubljanskigrad.si). Many other trails lead to the castle, and a funicular railway (charge) runs from **Krek Square** (Krekov trg). Although there has been a fortress here since medieval times, the castle you see today is the result of reconstruction following the 1511 earthquake. Through the centuries, the stronghold has been occupied by provincial leaders, and has been used as a garrison, a prison and a home for the poor; today it is one of several venues for the Ljubljana Summer Festival from June to mid-September (www.ljubljanafestival.si). The glass, steel and concrete restaurant in the central courtyard was installed as part of renovations in the 1980s. There are a couple of museums of varying interest within the castle's walls and towers, but the highlight is a climb to the top of the 150-step, nineteenth-century **Observation Tower**, from which there are stunning views over the city's terracotta rooftops to the Julian Alps. Below the tower, the **Virtual Museum** gives a twenty-minute multimedia presentation of the city's history.

The centre

The second bridge downstream from the Triple Bridge is Plečnik's pedestrian **Shoemaker's Bridge** (Čevljarski most), which leaps across to the modern city centre, a district of shops, offices and government buildings interspersed with public squares and museums. A short distance southwest of the bridge lies **French Revolution Square** (Trg francoske revolucije), which commemorates the period when Ljubljana was the capital of Napoleon's Illyrian Provinces (1809–13). On the south side, a former monastery belonging to the Order of Teutonic Knights has been converted by Plečnik into the open-air **Križanke Summer Theatre** (Križanke poletno gledališče) and is now a Summer Festival venue.

Just east of Križanke, at Gosposka 15, the **City Museum** (Mestni muzej; charge; www.mgml.si) offers an entertaining audiovisual presentation of Ljubljana's history, and also has a pleasant café.

North of Križanke, on Turjaška, is the **National and University Library** (Narodna i univerzitetna knjižnica or NUK; free, though entry to the reading room is restricted to members only), built in 1941 with a facade of rough grey stone and orange brick, punctuated with massive copper doors with horse-head handles. Many consider it Plečnik's greatest work. To the north is **Congress Square** (Kongresni trg), known as Star (Zvezda), a large green patch laid out for the Congress of the Holy Alliance in 1821 and overlooked by the **Philharmonic Hall** (Slovenska filharmonija; see page 103) from 1892.

East of Kongresni trg lies the less appealing **Republic Square** (Trg republike), and

The castle walls and observation tower

the colossal 1970s concrete Cankarjev Dom (see page 103), a multipurpose cultural centre. Here, too, is the 1959 **Parliament Building**, whose two-storey portal is stacked with statues of workers by Zdenko Kalin and Karl Putrih.

West of the busy thoroughfare of Slovenska lies the main conglomeration of museums. At Prešernova 24 the **National Gallery** (Narodna galerija; charge; www.ng-slo.si) displays Slovenian and European paintings from the Baroque period to the late nineteenth century. Close by, at Cankarjeva 15, the **Museum of Modern Art** (Moderna galerija; charge; www.mg-lj.si) showcases Slovenian twentieth-century paintings and sculptures, and also hosts the International Biennial of Graphic Arts in odd-numbered years. A few doors away at Prešernova 20, the **National Museum** (Narodni muzej; charge; www.nms.si) is filled with archaeological finds, most notably the Vače situla (see page 20). The building also houses the **Natural History Museum**.

The neo-Renaissance National Museum has archaeological finds

Tivoli Park

For a stroll amid rolling parkland, cross the busy Tivolska (subway near the Museum of Modern Art) to reach **Tivoli Park**, the city's major recreation area. An elegant white Baroque building shelters the **International Centre of**

Graphic Arts (Mednarodni grafični likovni center; charge; www.mglc-lj.si), housing regularly changing temporary modern art exhibitions. If you are travelling with children, you might consider the **Atlantis Water Park** (charge), 3km (2 miles) northeast of the city centre in **BTC City**, a vast shopping and entertainment complex.

> **NOTES**
>
> Look out for the local speciality, *kruhek*, decorated unleavened bread made with honey and cinnamon and shaped in wooden moulds. You will find these tasty treats for sale in several shops around town.

Northwest

Highlights

- **Škofja Loka**, see page 42
- **Kranj**, see page 43
- **Radovljica**, see page 44
- **Lake Bled**, see page 45
- **Vintgar Gorge**, see page 47
- **Triglav National Park**, see page 48
- **Lake Bohinj**, see page 48
- **Kranjska Gora to Trenta**, see page 51
- **Lepena Valley**, see page 53
- **Soča Valley**, see page 53
- **Kobarid**, see page 54
- **Nova Gorica**, see page 55
- **Dobrovo**, see page 55

With snowcapped alpine mountains, dense pine forests, emerald meadows and two beautiful lakes, the northwest is one of the finest corners of Slovenia. Heading northwest from Ljubljana, the first stop is lakeside Bled, the country's most-visited resort. From here the landscape becomes increasingly mountainous, with an average altitude of over 2000 metres (6500ft), taking in Triglav National Park and Kranjska Gora ski resort, before mellowing into Soča Valley's woodland, gorges and turquoise river.

Škofja Loka

From Ljubljana, on the A2 northwest to Bled, there is a popular detour to **Škofja Loka** ❷ on the River Sora, 19km (12 miles) from the city. During the Middle Ages this town was a regional centre for craftspeople and their guilds. Fortified in the fortified century, it was largely destroyed in an earthquake in 1511, and most of the painted facades and elegant churches date from sixteenth-century reconstruction. The old town centres on the **Town Square** (Mestni trg), the medieval marketplace, overlooked by the imposing **Town Hall** (Rotovž) and **Homan House** (Homan hiša), both a mix of Baroque and Gothic elements and decorated with sixteenth-century frescos. West of Town Square, the hilltop **castle** (grad), rebuilt in the sixteenth century after an earthquake, contains the **Loka Museum** (Loški muzej; charge; www.loski-muzej.si), with an interesting ethnographic section detailing the lives of local peasants in feudal times.

Tivoli Park

The town is known throughout Slovenia for the *Škofja Loka Passion* (*Škofjeloški Pasijon;* www.pasijon.si), a Passion play written in 1721, the oldest dramatic text in the Slovenian language. Performances were revived during the 1990s and take place every six years; it's next scheduled to be staged in 2026 and – with six hundred actors participating in twenty scenes, and four stages around town – it's quite a spectacle. Also, on the last weekend in June, a medieval street fair called the Venus Journey (Venerina pot) takes place, with local craftspeople demonstrating pottery, lacemaking and basketry on Town Square, plus street entertainers including fire eaters and swordsmen. The undulating green hills west of town are a haven for hiking and biking. Bikes can be rented from **Škofja Loka Tourist Information Centre** at Cankarjev trg 17 (www.visitskofjaloka.si). The centre can also supply a map of the 30km (19-mile) Loka cycle trail, leading through the surrounding villages.

Kranj

Located at the confluence of the Sava and Kokra rivers, 10km (6 miles) north of Škofja Loka (or 25km/15 miles northwest of Ljubljana via the A2), **Kranj** is Slovenia's fourth-largest town. Its uninspiring industrial suburbs belie a pleasant old town, at the heart of which is the **Main Square** (Glavni trg), rimmed by Gothic and Renaissance buildings. Nearby, at Prešernova 7, is the late-Gothic **Prešeren House** (Prešernova hiša; charge; www.gorenjski-muzej.si/lokacije/presernova-hisa), former home of Slovenia's best-known poet, France Prešeren (see page 22). The ground floor is devoted to temporary exhibitions, while on the first floor you can peer in his bedroom and office (he was a lawyer as well as a romantic poet), complete with early nineteenth-century furniture, plus a memorial museum displaying manuscripts, including translations of his works into Bengali and Chinese.

Tucked away in a narrow valley below the slopes of Jelovica, 11km (7 miles) northwest of Kranj, **Kropa** is a mining village

A quiet corner of Kranj, Slovenia's fourth-largest town

with a long history of wrought ironmaking. The **Iron Forging Museum** (Kovaški muzej; charge; https://mro.si/en/iron-forging-museum-kropa) traces the development of ironworking from the fifteenth century to its nineteenth-century decline, and the rise of handmade nails over the following hundred years. There is a section dedicated to the work of local master smith Joža Bertoncelj.

Radovljica

A sleepy provincial town, **Radovljica** is 21km (13 miles) northwest of Kranj. Honey production has been an important branch of agriculture in Slovenia since the eighteenth century, and Radovljica's unusual **Beekeeping Museum** (Čebelarski muzej; charge; https://mro.si/en/musem-of-apiculture), in a Baroque manor house on the main square at Linhartov trg 1, tells the story of beekeeping and the indigenous Grey Carniolan bee. Painted wooden beehive panels are a local folk art, intended to enable each beekeeper to identify his hives. Some depict scenes from the Bible and others capture amusing moments from everyday rural life or folklore: look out for the image of a tailor being pursued by an angry giant snail. Next door to the Beekeeping Museum, *Gostilna Lectar* (see page 121) is a highly regarded restaurant, perfect for sampling traditional Slovenian dishes.

Lake Bled

Cradled in a basin surrounded by the rugged, snowcapped Julian Alps, **Bled** ❸ is Slovenia's most-visited resort, 50km (30 miles) northwest of Ljubljana. The jewel of this idyllic hideaway is the emerald-green Lake Bled, inset with a small island and church and guarded by a clifftop castle. Tourism took root here in 1855, when European aristocrats began visiting the lake to enjoy its efficacious thermal waters and the invigorating alpine air. Today, busloads descend from all over Europe, but the lake and its setting remain undeniably beautiful. Hotels and guesthouses cater for every budget, and there are bathing facilities, and boats and bicycles to rent. It's even possible to host a wedding ceremony in the castle.

Despite its popularity, few people venture far from town, and so it's easy to escape the crowds by walking the 6km (4-mile) perimeter of the lake along a waterside path lined with lime trees, horse chestnuts and weeping willows. A highlight is clambering up the steep hill of Mala Osojnica for perfect views of the lake, the island and the castle on the opposite shore.

The ramparts of **Bled Castle** ❹ (Blejski grad; charge; www.blejski-grad.si), built on a rocky outcrop 100 metres (330ft) above the water, also offer impressive views of the lake. Dating from the eleventh century, the castle's present appearance is largely seventeenth century. Inside, the **Castle Museum** (Grajski muzej) displays archaeological finds, period furniture and armoury.

In the middle of the western half of the lake is **Bled Island** (Blejski otok), where an elegant church and bell tower poke through the trees. To visit this idyllic speck, either rent a rowing boat or take a guided trip on a *pletnja* (like a Venetian gondola) from the landing station opposite Vila Prešeren, close to the centre of town. A continuous flight of 99 steps lead from the island's quay up to the seventeenth-century Baroque **Church of the Assumption**, a popular place for weddings, partly because the early Slavs built a pagan temple to Živa – their goddess of love and fertility – on the site, and partly because it's a gorgeous spot. The highlight of the ceremony is a challenge for the groom to carry the bride up all 99 steps without stopping. The adjoining fifteenth-century belltower

Lake Bled with Bled Island, reached by rowing boat or pletnja

is said to bring good luck to those who ring the bell.

On the north bank of the lake, directly beneath the castle, is the **Castle Swimming Grounds** (Grajsko kopališče), while on the west side of the lake, the **Rowing Centre** (Veslaški center; www.veslaska-zveza.si) organises the Bled International Regatta each year in mid-June, attracting world-class rowers. Nearby, the free public bathing area with manicured lawns running down to the water is a pleasant place to swim and sunbathe.

NOTES

Strictly for adrenaline junkies, the Dolinka Zipline (https://zipline-dolinka.si) is Europe's longest, with four kilometres' worth across seven different lines which span the Dolinka river, just outside Bled. If you've ever fancied soaring through the trees among pristine mountain scenery, this is ideal.

On the south bank, a twenty-minute walk from town, set in manicured gardens, **Vila Bled** was largely built by the Yugoslav royal family in the early twentieth century as a summer mansion. Tito used it as a retreat and to entertain world leaders, including Indira Ghandi and Nikita Khrushchev. Since 1984 it has been a luxury hotel. The Royal Bled Golf Club (www.royalbled.com), 3km (2 miles) east of Bled, is considered one of the most beautiful in Europe (see page 97).

Vintgar Gorge

The spectacular **Vintgar Gorge** ❺ (Blejski vintgar; charge; www.vintgar.si) lies 4km (2.5 miles) north of Bled. Carved by the River Radovna and flanked by rocky outcrops and birch woods, it was first explored in 1891. A series of suspended wooden walkways and bridges crisscross the length of the 1600m (1-mile) gorge, passing over thundering waterfalls and rapids and culminating with the 13m (43ft) -high Šum Waterfall (Slap Šum).

Triglav National Park

Triglav National Park attracts 2.5 million visitors a year. Its stunning alpine mountains, valleys, lakes and rivers offer a dramatic backdrop to outdoor activities such as hiking, cycling and white-water rafting, plus skiing in winter. There are 33 settlements in the park and a population of 2400. Protected animals include brown bears, lynx and golden eagles.

Lake Bohinj

While Lake Bled is postcard-perfect, its sister lake 26km (16 miles) southwest in Triglav National Park is larger and wilder, set in an unspoilt alpine landscape of pine woods and lush meadows speckled with wildflowers, against a backdrop of snowcapped mountains. Unlike Bled, **Lake Bohinj** ❻ (Bohinjsko Jezero) is almost untouched by modern development; building on the shores of the lake is prohibited. Bohinj is an excellent base for hiking, with a number of well-kept mountain paths.

At **Ribčev Laz**, you can find *Hotel Jezero*, a Tourist Information Centre (at No. 48) stocking local hiking maps, and several agencies catering for adventure sports and hiring bicycles, kayaks and canoes. It is possible to swim near here; the best places lie along the northeast corner of the lake. Alternatively, keen walkers may embark on a 12km (8-mile) hike around the perimeter of the lake. Ribčev Laz also has the elegant whitewashed medieval **Church of St John the Baptist** (Cerkev svetega Janeza; charge; www.janez-krstnik-bohinj.si), decorated with fifteenth- and sixteenth-century biblical frescos on the inside and a large St Christopher outside.

From the small quay opposite the church, regular boats (charge; www.bohinj.si/en/panoramic-boat) shuttle visitors from Ribčev Laz to Camp Zlatorog in the small holiday village of **Ukanc** at the west end of the lake. Alternatively, the road along the south shore also leads to Ukanc, 4.5km (2.5 miles) away. From here, a marked footpath heads west to the popular **Savica Waterfall** (Slap Savica), a

97-metre (318ft) cascade of water thundering into a deep gorge, which is reached by a steep set of steps. The most popular hiking route up **Mount Triglav**, Slovenia's highest mountain (2864 metres/9396ft), begins in Ukanc. South of Ukanc, the **Vogel Cable Car** ❼ (charge; www.vogel.si) takes visitors up to the **Vogel Ski Centre**, at an altitude of 1535 metres (5036ft). From here, the view of the lake and the surrounding mountains is superb.

Back at the east end of the lake, northeast of Ribčev Laz, a scattering of peaceful alpine farming villages offer rustic restaurants, rooms to let and a couple of small museums. In a nineteenth-century dairy in **Stara Fužina**, a short walk north of Ribčev Laz, the **Alpine Dairy Museum** (Planšarski muzej; charge;

Triglav National Park

www.gorenjski-muzej.si/lokacije/planšarski-muzej) presents the history of dairy farming and cheesemaking in the area. In **Studor** (1.5km/1 mile east of Stara Fužina), the **Oplen House** (Oplenova hiša; charge; www.gorenjski-muzej.si/lokacije/oplenova-hisa) is a typical nineteenth-century stone-and-wood farmhouse, with a 'black kitchen' for smoking ham, a loom for weaving and original farm tools. The well-signed **Mrcina Ranč** (www.ranc-mrcina.com) is a riding centre in Studor with Icelandic ponies for trekking.

Kranjska Gora to Trenta

Northwest of Bled, close to both the Austrian and Italian borders, **Kranjska Gora** is Slovenia's biggest and best-known skiing resort

Wild and unspoilt Lake Bohinj in Triglav National Park

MOUNT TRIGLAV

With its distinctive three peaks (Triglav means 'three heads'), Triglav enchanted the early Slavs, who believed it to be the home of a three-headed god who ruled the sky, the earth and the underworld. Today it is the symbol of Slovenia and is featured on the country's flag. National pride decrees that every true Slovene should reach the 2864-metre (9396ft) peak of the mountain at least once in their lifetime, and there is an annual climb of '100 Women on Mount Triglav' to highlight the role of women. The ascent can be very demanding and is usually broken by at least one overnight stay in a mountain hut.

(see page 92) and also a good base for hiking in summer. Each year in March, Kranjska Gora hosts the Planica Ski Jumping World Cup Championship, and it was here that Finland's Matti Hautamäki leapt an amazing 231 metres (758ft) in 2003, a world record that held for two years. The current record is 254.5 metres and was also set here, by Slovenian ski jumper Domen Prevc in 2025. The resort is well equipped with big hotels and family-run guesthouses, though there are few cultural attractions besides the **Liznjek House** (Liznjekova domačija; charge; www.gmj.si/liznjekova-domacija-kranjska-gora), an eighteenth-century farmhouse devoted to an ethnographic exhibition. The **Kranjska Gora Bike Park** (charge; https://ski-kranjska-gora.com/en/summer/bike-park) offers exciting downhill tracks plus mountain bikes to rent.

Between Kranjska Gora and Trenta, the spectacular **Vršič Pass** ❽ is a 25km (15-mile) stretch of hairpin bends commanding stunning views and rising to an altitude of 1611 metres (5285ft). The pass was built during World War I to enable supplies to reach the Austrian army fighting along the Soča Front. It is often blocked by heavy snow during winter.

The village of **Trenta**, 25km (15 miles) south of Kranjska Gora, is worth a stop to look in the **Triglav National Park Information**

THE SOČA FRONT

When Italy entered World War I in 1915, intending to advance east into Austro-Hungarian territory, the River Soča (Isonzo in Italian) became the natural front line, running some 90km (55 miles) south from Bovec almost to Trieste on the Adriatic coast. After 29 months of fighting, the decisive battle, the 'Miracle at Kobarid', took place in 1917, in which the combined forces of the Central Powers defeated the Italian army. Fighting in the Soča Valley resulted in the deaths of an estimated one million soldiers and civilians, plus a mass exodus of inhabitants from the area, very few of whom ever returned. Ernest Hemingway, who was working as a volunteer ambulance driver for the Italian forces, based his novel *A Farewell to Arms* on this experience.

Centre, housed in the Trenta Lodge (www.tnp.si), which has an informative multimedia presentation of the park's geology and indigenous flora and fauna. The centre also offers guided hiking tours following the 20km (12-mile) Soča Trail.

Close by, the **Juliana Alpine Botanical Garden** (Alpinum Juliana; charge; www.juliana.pms-lj.si) specialises in high-altitude Alpine flora. Founded in 1925 by Albert Bois de Chesne, most of the plants it displays are indigenous to the region, though there is a small area reserved for non-endemic species from the French Pyrenees and Caucasus. The garden is at its most beautiful in May and the beginning of June.

Lepena Valley

Further southwest is the road junction for the **Lepena Valley** on the left between Trenta and Bovec. Here, on a green plateau overlooking the Soča Valley, you will find the idyllic **Pristava Lepena**, a low-key holiday village combining traditional wooden Alpine cottages, a riding centre with Lipizzaner horses for trekking, and a good restaurant.

Soča Valley

Bovec, 35km (22 miles) southwest of Kranjska Gora, marks the beginning of the rocky gorges and dense pine forests of the remote **Soča Valley**. The area is a popular destination for adventure-sports enthusiasts, who enjoy kayaking, canoeing, rafting and canyoning on the turquoise **River Soča**, which flows south as far as Nova Gorica (after which it runs into Italy and becomes known as the Isonzo). **Bovec** started out as a ski resort (see page 92), but now caters for adventure sports from May to September. Due to a series of natural disasters, including a fire and two earthquakes, plus the destruction of World War I, the town centre is modern and functional but offers no notable cultural attractions. However, 6km (4 miles) southwest

Alpine landscape around Kranjska Gora

Kayaking on the River Soča

of Bovec, the **Boka Waterfall** (Slap Boka), in two stages of 38 metres (125ft) and 106 metres (348ft), is impressive enough to warrant a stop.

Kobarid

The peaceful Alpine town of **Kobarid** ❾, 21km (13 miles) south of Bovec, lies in the shadow of Mount Krn (2244 metres/7360ft). Its cultural attraction is the **Kobarid Museum** (Kobariški muzej, Gregorčičeva 10; charge; www.kobariski-muzej.si) in the eighteenth-century Mašer House. This anti-war collection gives a thought-provoking account of the fighting that took place along the banks of the River Soča during World War I (see page 52). Exhibits include photos, maps, scale models, flags, military uniforms and arms. The museum runs the 5km (3-mile) **Kobarid History Trail** (Kobariška zgodovinska pot) and can provide a self-guiding pamphlet and map. The well-marked path crosses green meadows and a stone canyon to take in sites related to World War I, including the Italian frontline where it is still possible to make out the trenches, and the Italian War Memorial, a monumental octagonal mausoleum holding the bodies of more than seven thousand Italian soldiers killed during the fighting. It starts and finishes at **Trg svobode**, the main square.

Kobarid's other big pull for visitors is its river-based activities. There are a number of agencies based here that arrange rafting, canyoning, kayaking and canoeing trips from May to September.

Trout-fishing enthusiasts can pick up a permit from *Hotel Hvala* on the main square. The season runs from April to October.

Nova Gorica

Best known for its 24-hour casinos, **Nova Gorica**, 53km (33 miles) south of Kobarid, is a 'new town' on the border with Italy. After World War II, the predominantly Slovenian-speaking town of Gorizia was awarded to Italy. To compensate for the loss, Tito set about building a new town (Nova Gorica means New Gorizia) with the designs of Slovenian architect Edo Ravnikar. The result: the concrete apartment blocks and landscaped green parks of today.

Despite its interesting past, Nova Gorica is a relatively dull place. The main attraction is its numerous casinos, popular with Italians who hop over the border in busloads daily. Slovenia's largest casino, and reputedly one of the biggest in Europe, occupies the ground floor of **Hotel Casino Perla**. Open all day every day, it has ninety gaming tables for roulette, blackjack, poker and other games, and 888 slot machines.

NOTES

For more than forty years Nova Gorica and Gorizia were separated by tough border control. Everything changed on 30 April 2004, the day before Slovenia's entry into the EU, with celebrations in Piazza Transalpina to commemorate the start of free movement. Once divided by a wire mesh barrier, the piazza is now a symbol of European unification. A mosaic has been made including fragments of the numbers 57/15 that formerly marked the border stone in the centre of the square.

Dobrovo

The region of **Goriška Brda** is known for its undulating hills planted with vineyards and its fine cellars stocking red and white wines. Close to the Italian border, its largest settlement and chief wine-producing centre is **Dobrovo**, 16km (10 miles) northwest of Nova Gorica.

Kobarid Museum remembers the frontline in World War I

The town's main sight is the white sixteenth-century Renaissance **Dobrovo Castle** housing the **Dobrovo Castle Museum Collection** (Muzejska zbirka grad Dobrovo; charge; www.goriskimuzej.si/stalne-zbirke/grad-dobrovo). On the first floor, next to the Knights' Hall, the nineteenth-century cultural history collection is worth a look, as are the prints by local twentieth-century artist Zoran Mušič on the second floor.

However, most people come to the castle to visit **Vinoteka Brda** (www.vinotekabrda.si), which offers wine tasting in a stone-vault cellar in the castle courtyard.

Close by at Zadružna cesta 9, the **Klet Brda wine cellars** (http://klet-brda.si) make another fine venue for wine tasting, being the largest cellar in Slovenia, storing a staggering 18-million litres (4-million gallons) of the good stuff.

Southwest: inland

Highlights

- **Idrija**, see below
- **The Karst region**, see page 58

The southwest is made up of two contrasting but complementary regions: the coast and the Karst region.

Slovenia has just 47km (30 miles) of seaboard, but it is well worth seeing for its pretty ports, enriched with Venetian-style architecture, and for the country's most popular seaside resort, Portorož. The main calling card of the inland Karst region, an attractive region of steep, cultivated valleys, is its extraordinary labyrinth of underground caves and the world-renowned Lipizzaner horses.

Idrija

From Ljubljana, the A1 leads southwest to Koper. En route, a possible detour is **Idrija**, 60km (38 miles) from the capital, cradled in a valley at the confluence of the rivers Idrijca and Nikova. Mercury was discovered here in 1490, and when production reached its peak in the second half of the eighteenth century, Idrija was providing thirteen percent of the world market. However, by the late twentieth century mercury was regarded as a serious pollutant, capable of causing brain damage. The world price plummeted, and the last mine closed in 1999. Tours of **Idrija Mercury Mine** (Kosovelova ulica 3; charge; www.cudhg-idrija.si) begin with an audiovisual presentation about the history of the town and the mine, after which visitors don helmets and jackets to embark on an atmospheric 1200-metre (0.75-mile) loop through the mine and a unique eighteenth-century underground chapel.

The town is dominated by the sixteenth-century **Gewerkenegg Castle** (Grad Gewerkenegg), built as the mine's administrative centre, and now the **Town Museum** (Mestni muzej; charge; www.

muzej-idrija-cerkno.si), giving visitors an insight into the history of Idrija's mercury-mining industry. There is also a permanent gallery collection comprising of prints and paintings by renowned Slovene and Italian artists, as well as a section on the craft of lacemaking. A lace school was established in 1876, and Idrija is known throughout Slovenia for the art, which is still alive today.

Each year in late June, Idrija hosts a ten-day Lacemaking Festival (Čipkarski festival; www.festivalidrijskecipke.si) with displays and events all around the town. On **Mestni trg**, the main square, there is a cluster of small boutiques where you can buy lace all year-round. While you're in Idrija, call by **Restavracija Barbara** (see page 121) to try the local speciality, *žlikrofi*, potato balls spiked with marjoram and wrapped in pasta.

The clock tower of Idrija's Gewerkenegg Castle

The Karst region

Lying between Postojna and the coast, the dramatic Karst region is a wild, barren, rocky landscape interspersed with vineyards, pine woods and rural limestone villages. The word *karst* (*kras* in Slovenian) originated here and has since been adopted as the global term for the geological phenomenon characterised by sinkholes, underground streams and caves with stalactites and stalagmites, which occurs in limestone areas.

Postojna Cave

Europe's most-visited cave, and probably your first choice for a cave tour, is near the town of **Postojna**, 44km (27 miles) southwest of Ljubljana. **Postojna Cave** ⑩ (Postojnska jama; charge; www.postojnska-jama.eu) comprises 20km (13 miles) of halls and passages, of which a quarter is open to the public. The ninety-minute tour starts with a train ride through 3.5km (2 miles) of ingeniously lit tunnels and grottoes dripping with stalactites and stalagmites. The remaining 1.5km (1 mile) covered on foot takes in the stunning **Concert Hall**, which can hold audiences of up to 10,000 and is occasionally used for concerts. At Christmas it becomes a 'living crib' accompanied by carol singing.

The **Vivarium**, close to the cave entrance, shows a short film about the karst and displays live specimens of cave fauna, including the bizarre 'human fish' inside an aquarium (see box). It is amazing to think that anything at all can live in these conditions.

Predjama Castle

The magically beautiful **Predjama Castle** ⑪ (Predjamski Grad; charge; www.postojnska-jama.eu) lies near the village of Predjama, 7km (4 miles) northwest of Postojna Cave. Built into the rocks of a sheer cliff face, it dates back to the thirteenth century, though its present Renaissance appearance is largely the result of sixteenth-century alterations. Inside, several rooms are furnished in period style, the stairs to the upper floors are carved in solid bedrock, and below the castle there's a **cave**.

Lake Cerknica

Lake Cerknica, described as the 'disappearing' lake, is another of the region's typical karst features. This unusual natural phenomenon is 8km (5 miles) east of Postojna. It vanishes completely in the summer, but from October to June it fills up with water, and is at its largest in spring, when it is around 10km (6 miles) long and 5km

> **NOTES**
>
> The *Proteus anguinus*, known in Slovenia as the 'human fish', is a flesh-pink amphibious salamander endemic to the karst caves. Growing to about 25–30cm (10–12ins), it can live for up to a hundred years, many spent in total darkness. With no eyes but a keen sense of smell, it feeds on crustacea and worms, although its very slow metabolism allows it to survive for several years without eating at all.

(3 miles) wide, but never deeper than 5 metres (16ft). Locals enjoy fishing and windsurfing here, and it's also a popular birding spot.

Škocjan Caves

The UNESCO-protected **Škocjan Caves** ⓬ (Škocjanske jame; charge; www.park-skocjanske-jame.si) lie 26km (16 miles) southwest of Postojna, and 5km (3 miles) southeast of Divača. The ninety-minute tour takes visitors on foot through 2.5km (1.5 miles) of the total 6km (4-mile) network. It's chilly and can be uneven underfoot. The main sights are the **Silent Cave**, decorated with stalagmites and stalactites, and the unforgettable **Murmuring Cave**, an underground gorge some 300 metres long, 60 metres wide and 100 metres high (980 x 200 x 330ft), carved by the emerald-green River Reka that roars and echoes in the cave. It is crossed by the narrow Cerkvenik Bridge, which is suspended a hair-raising 45 metres (150ft) above the water. Close by, the well-marked **Škocjan Educational Trail** runs through the Škocjan Caves park, introducing visitors to the surrounding natural and cultural features of the area.

Lipica Stud Farm

The peaceful green pastures and whitewashed stables of the **Lipica Stud Farm** ⓭ (Kobilarna Lipica; charge; www.lipica.org) lie 7km (4 miles) south of Divača off the A1. The birthplace of the Lipizzaner white horses was founded in 1580 by the Habsburgs, who wanted to create an elegant cart- and saddlehorse for their court. They imported Barbary horses from Spain, which had been brought to Europe by the Moors from North Africa, and crossed them with Arab horses and local Karst ponies. The result was the splendid Lipizzaner, which became the original horses of the famous Spanish Riding School in Vienna. In season, visitors can watch the incredible dressage performances. Riding lessons are available on request.

Štanjel

The medieval fortified hilltop settlement of **Štanjel**, 18km (11 miles) northwest of Divača, is one of the most beautiful villages in Slovenia. The ancient walls, entered through an arched gate, wrap around a huddle of stone cottages and the sixteenth-century Baroque-Renaissance **Štanjel Castle** (Grad Štanjel). It was badly damaged during World War II, but one wing houses the **Lojze Spacal Gallery** (Galerija Lojze Spacala; charge; www.visitstanjel.si/en/the-lojze-spacal-gallery), displaying an impressive collection of karst-inspired paintings and graphics by Trieste-born Spacal. The ticket is also valid for the nearby fifteenth-century stone **Karst House** (Kraška hiša), a classic example of local folk architecture.

The dramatically situated Predjama Castle

Ice surfing on Lake Cerknica

Hrastovlje

The tiny Romanesque **Church of the Holy Trinity** (Cerkev svete Trojice; charge; https://visitkoper.si/en/sight/hrastovlje-2) at **Hrastovlje** ⓮, 31km (19 miles) south of Divača, is nestled in sixteenth-century ramparts, built against the Turks. The interior is covered with fifteenth-century frescos depicting biblical scenes, such as the *Creation* and the *Last Judgement*. Painted in 1490 by Janez iz Kastva, they were only rediscovered beneath several layers of whitewash in the 1950s. The best-known is the *Danse Macabre* (Dance of Death), showing how, regardless of social status, we are all equal in death. There is also a *Calendar Cycle*, portraying the past duties and rituals that took place every month of the year, and an informative twenty-minute taped commentary in several languages.

The coast

Highlights

- **Koper**, see page 63
- **Izola and Strunjan**, see page 65
- **Piran**, see page 65
- **Portorož**, see page 67
- **Sečovlje**, see page 68

The scenic Slovenian coast stretches 47km (26 miles) between Croatia and Italy, where budget airlines deposit visitors at Trieste. The tideless waters are clean and clear, and ideal for swimming. The local dialect, cuisine and architecture are distinctly Italian, the legacy of Venetian rule. The tourist centres of Portorož (Portorose in Italian) and Piran (Pirano) are packed with hotels, restaurants and marinas, while the industrial port of Koper (Capodistria), 105km (63 miles) southwest of Ljubljana, is often overlooked but has a magnificent historic centre.

NOTES

Lipizzaner horses are born black or brown and turn white around the age of seven. They stand 15–15.3hh (1.55–1.58 metres/61–2in), have long powerful backs and strong muscular necks, and can be trained to perform intricate dressage steps. Slovenia's entry to the Eurozone was marked by the Lipizzaner horse on the 20-cent coin.

Koper

Koper ⓯ is Slovenia's main port. Tourists often pass it by, considering it too industrial, but the medieval **old town** contains some of Slovenia's most beautiful buildings from the Venetian era. Hard to imagine today, the city was once an island cast adrift from the mainland until a landfill connected the two in the nineteenth century. Koper was founded by the ancient Greeks as Aegida, renamed Capris by the Romans, then became Byzantine Justinopolis. In 1279 it was seized by the Venetians, who made it the capital of Venetian Istria, hence its Italian name, 'Capo d'Istria'. By the sixteenth century the population had surged to 10,000.

Koper's most impressive monuments are found in the well-preserved old town on **Tito Square** (Titov trg). On the north side stands the seventeenth-century Venetian-Gothic **loggia** (Loža), whose ground-floor *Loggia Café* is a perfect spot for coffee while enjoying the view across the square. Opposite the loggia, the **Praetorian Palace** (Pretorska palača) is a hotch-potch of Venetian-Gothic and Renaissance styles. It was built as the residence of Koper's *podesta* (mayor), and the seat of the Grand Council. A tourist information centre occupies the ground floor. On the square's eastern side, the twelfth-century **Cathedral of the Assumption** (Stolnica Marijinega vnebovzetja; free) again combines Venetian-Gothic and Renaissance elements. Visitors can climb the 36-metre (118ft) bell tower (charge) for stunning views over the Gulf of Trieste. Behind the cathedral is the twelfth-century circular baptistery.

West of Tito Square, the **Koper Regional Museum** (Pokrajinski muzej Koper, Kidričeva 19; charge; www.pokrajinskimuzejkoper.si) displays an assortment of stone carvings from local churches, period furniture and paintings, plus a fine copy of the *Danse Macabre* from the Holy Trinity in Hrastovlje (see page 62).

East of Tito Square, close to the former town walls, the **Ethnological Collection** (Etnološka zbirka, Gramšijev trg 4; charge; www.pokrajinski muzejkoper.si) is housed in a fourteenth-century Venetian-Gothic building. The exhibition highlights the local use of stone in building and sculpture from the seventeenth century onwards.

The Church of the Holy Trinity

Izola and Strunjan

Izola, 6km (4 miles) south of Koper, is an easy-going fishing town, built on a small peninsula jutting out to sea. As the name suggests, the town was once an island; it was joined to the mainland in the nineteenth century. The old town is a knot of narrow, crooked streets lined with Venetian-style, pastel-coloured buildings. Although appealing, there's little in the way of cultural interest, and most people come here simply to enjoy the sea and sunshine or to sail from the large marina on the edge of town.

Lying between Izola and Piran, **Strunjan** is a 4km (2.5 mile) stretch of coast backed by dramatic cliffs, giving onto a pebble beach popular with nudists. Strunjan Bay was once an important area for the saltmaking industry, and the saltpans can still be made out today.

West of Strunjan is a campsite and the *Strunjan Health Resort*, offering therapeutic body treatments using mud from the former saltpans. The 160ha (395-acre) **Strunjan Nature Reserve** includes a 200m (650ft) -wide coastal water belt to protect marine species.

Piran

Piran ⓰ is Slovenia's most beautiful coastal town. Sitting compact on a small, pointed peninsula, the old town is a huddle of pastel-painted Venetian-Gothic buildings watched over by a hilltop church. The town's name, derived from the Greek *pyr*, nods to the fire that was lit on the tip of the peninsula to guide galleys into the port at nearby Aegida (Koper), 10km (6 miles) away. In the fifth century AD, Romans fleeing to the coast to escape the Huns settled here.

For some five hundred years, between 1283 and 1797, Piran was under Venetian rule, which produced splendid buildings and a proud maritime status. The Republic was supplied with salt from the nearby saltpans. Subsequent relative neglect under the Habsburgs preserved the charming medieval atmosphere.

Koper's Praetorian Palace, where the Grand Council sat

Today, Piran's main public meeting point is the white marble, oval-shaped **Tartini Square** (Tartinijev trg), which was the inner harbour until 1864 when it was filled in. It is named after the musician Giuseppe Tartini, and his bronze statue is at its centre. He was born in the yellow house (No. 7), where the **Tartini Memorial Room** occupies the first floor (Tartinijeva spominska soba; https://pomorskimuzej.si/en/giuseppe-tartini-memorial-room). It contains his death mask, violin and music manuscripts.

Tartini Square opens onto the fishing harbour and, beyond, the **Prešernovo nabrežje** promenade, which is lined with seafood restaurants. On the hill above town is the seventeenth-century Baroque **Church of St George** (Cerkev svetega Jurija). Its freestanding belltower resembles a smaller version of Venice's San Marco campanile. If you are lucky enough to find it open during your visit, be sure to climb to the top for stunning views over the Gulf of Trieste.

A few steps west of Tartini Square is Piran's **Aquarium** (Kidričevo nabrežje 4; charge; https://aquariumpiran.si). Here, a series of well-lit pools exhibits various flora and fauna from the Adriatic Sea. On the other side of the harbour is another marine life-focused exhibition, the **Shell Museum** (Muzej školjk; Cankarjevo nabrežje 1; charge; www.svet-skoljk.si), a small place with an extensive collection of shells, starfish and crustaceans from local and further afield waters.

Overlooking the harbour at Cankarjevo nabrežje 3, the **Sergej Mašera Maritime Museum** (Pomorski muzej Sergej Mašera; charge; www.pomorskimuzej.si/en/gabrielli-palace) traces Piran's naval history and maritime past.

Portorož

Piran is connected to **Portorož** by a coastal promenade, overlooked by a string of large modern hotels. People have been visiting the 'port of roses' for health therapies since the thirteenth

GIUSEPPE TARTINI

Violinist and composer Giuseppe Tartini (1692–1770) was born in Piran and attended school in nearby Koper. Against the wishes of his parents, who wanted him to become a Franciscan monk, he went to Padua in Italy to study law. At 18 he eloped with Elizabetta Premazone, the Bishop of Padua's niece. After three years the couple were found. To escape prosecution Tartini fled to the Convent of St Francis in Assisi where he started playing the violin. Pardoned, he returned to Padua to set up a violin school, attracting students from all over Europe. He composed more than 130 pieces for violin. The best known, a solo sonata called *The Devil's Trill*, was written after he dreamed the devil was playing the instrument. He is buried next to his wife in Padua.

century, when Benedictine monks started treating diseases with the seawater and mineral-rich mud from local saltpans. In the late nineteenth century, Portorož established itself as a wellness centre and an aristocratic tourist resort.

Today it is a commercial resort, with a beach of imported sand lined with sunloungers and parasols, and a row of upmarket hotels offering health and beauty treatments.

Sečovlje

South of Portorož, close to the Croatian border, on the **Sečovlje Saltpans**, lies the **Saltworks Museum** (Muzej solinarstva; charge; www.pomorskimuzej.si/en/the-museum-of-salt-making). Set

Beautiful Venetian-era Piran on Slovenia's coast

in a flat, wet landscape straddled by dykes, these pans were begun in the thirteenth century and covered 650ha (1600 acres). They were abandoned in 1967. Each year, local saltworkers left their winter homes to live in stone cottages on the saltpans from spring to early autumn. Three of the original four hundred cottages have been restored to form the museum, and tools used for work in the saltpans are displayed here.

Violinist Giuseppe Tartini's statue in Tartini Square, Piran

Northeast

Highlights

- **Kamnik and Velika planina**, see page 70
- **Logar Valley**, see page 71
- **Celje**, see page 71
- **Rogaška Slatina**, see page 73
- **Maribor**, see page 74
- **Ptuj**, see page 76
- **Wine roads around Ptuj**, see page 78
- **Murska Sobota**, see page 79
- **Moravske Toplice**, see page 80

A world apart from the Mediterranean seascapes and alpine mountains of western Slovenia, the northeast is typically Central

European. Here, the influences of Vienna and Budapest are apparent in the architecture, the cuisine and the wines. The main cities are Maribor, Ptuj and Celje, each one with a castle, bearing witness to the centuries lived in fear of Turkish attack.

The region also offers wine cellars open for tasting, wine roads leading through rural vineyard country, and several modern thermal spas.

Kamnik and Velika planina

From Ljubljana, the A1 leads northeast to Maribor, then on towards the Hungarian border. En route, a popular detour is **Kamnik**, 23km (14 miles) northeast of the capital. A pretty medieval town below the Kamnik Alps (Kamniške Alpe), Kamnik is a popular base for hikers due to the proximity of Velika planina. In the handsome Renaissance-Baroque **Zaprice Castle** (Zaprice grad, really a grand manor house) is the **Kamnik Museum** (Kamniški muzej; charge; www.muzej-kamnik-on.net), presenting the way people in the region lived in the nineteenth century. It's also worth a stop at the attractive **Little Castle** (Mali Grad; Parmova ulica 4; charge), which sits atop a small hillock in the town centre: if it's open, you can admire remnants of medieval frescoes inside the chapel; if it's not, the vantage point affords great views of the mountains to the north.

Velika planina (www.velikaplanina.si) is a green mountain plateau 5km (3 miles) north of Kamnik, accessible by cable car and ski lift. Traditionally, the area was given over to dairy farming, but due to its natural beauty this has been superseded by tourism.

From spring to autumn visitors hike through the flower-carpeted alpine meadows, dotted with small settlements of wooden, shingle-roof circular huts. In winter, skiing and night-time sledging are possible.

Volčji Potok Arboretum (4km/2.5 miles south of Kamnik; charge; www.arboretum.si) occupies beautifully landscaped grounds, and is home to more than 3500 species and varieties of conifers, deciduous trees and wild herbaceous plants. There is a neat French garden and informal English park, plus an 18-hole golf course.

Logar Valley

The **Logar Valley** ⓱ (Logarska dolina) is a stunning green glacial valley 34km (21 miles) northeast of Kamnik, with rugged peaks nudging 2000 metres (6560 ft) on each side. The clearly marked, 7km (4.5-mile) **Logar Valley Trail** wends to the 90m (295ft) -high **Rinka Waterfall** (Slap Rinka). On the way, the route traces the story of the glacial origins of the valley, its wildlife and the way local people have lived over the centuries. The information hut at the entry point can supply visitors with details about organised hiking tours, horse riding, rock climbing and mountain biking.

The wooden huts and alpine meadows of Velika planina

Celje

Slovenia's third-largest city was built by the Romans in the first century AD as Celeia, a prosperous, densely populated walled town on the Roman road from Aquileia to Pannonia on the River Savinja 74km (46 miles) northeast of Ljubljana. **Celje** (pronounced *tselyeh*) enjoyed a second period of glory as a principality under the wealthy Counts of Celje during the Middle Ages. In 1456 it came under Habsburg rule, where it remained until 1918.

Today, despite its unattractive industrial suburbs, it warrants a day's sightseeing. The ruins of the medieval **Old Castle** (Stari grad; charge; www.visitcelje.eu/product/celje-castle), perched on a 4000m (1300ft) -high rock, 2km (1 mile) southeast of town, is Celje's best-known landmark and the largest castle complex in Slovenia. Built by the Counts of Celje, one of Central Europe's most powerful noble families, the ruins are sheltered within extensive walls. The most intact building is the fourteenth-century, four-storey **Frederick's Tower** (Friderikov stolp), which offers excellent views. In summer, medieval re-enactments are staged here.

Celje, the third-largest city

Celje's other sights lie in the old town, a pleasant provincial jumble of Renaissance, Baroque and twentieth-century buildings and squares. At Prešernova 17, the **Museum of Recent History** (Muzej novejše zgodovine; charge; www.muzej-nz-ce.si) examines life in twentieth-century Celje. The Children's Museum here has toys and prams, plus a workshop and playroom.

Close to the river in a fine Renaissance building, at Muzejski trg 1, the **Celje Regional Museum** (Pokrajinski muzej Celje; charge; www.pokmuz-ce.si) is noted for the **Celje**

Ceiling, decorated with early seventeenth-century frescos. A haunting standout of the rest of the eclectic exhibition is the collection of skulls of eighteen Counts of Celje.

For evidence of Celje's Roman past, visit **Šempeter**, 12km (8 miles) west of town. Here, along a 300m (1000ft) -long section of the Roman road that once ran between Ljubljana and Celje, is the **Roman Necropolis** (Rimska nekropola; charge; www.td-sempeter.si), which has well-preserved marble tombs of local Roman dignitaries from the first to third century AD.

Thirsty travellers might swing by **Laško**, 11km (8 miles) south of Celje, renowned throughout Slovenia for churning out the country's favourite beer, Laško Zlatorog. To request a tour of the brewery, contact the Laško Tourist Board (https://lasko.info). Each year in mid-July, the five-day Beer and Flowers (Pivo in Cvetje) festival pays homage to the much-loved beverage. The town is also known for its thermal springs, and visitors come here to enjoy the indoor and outdoor pools, as well as the saunas.

Rogaška Slatina

Slovenia's oldest and most-visited spa town, **Rogaška Slatina** 18 is 36km (23 miles) east of Celje, close to the Croatian border. During the nineteenth century, the mineral-rich thermal waters of this elegant retreat attracted an illustrious list of European aristocrats, including the Habsburgs, the Bourbons and the Bonapartes. Today it offers luxurious health and beauty therapies, as well as being one of the top spas in Central Europe for the treatment of metabolic disorders.

The town centres on Zdraviliški trg, a large square with neatly kept gardens, overlooked by nineteenth-century Neoclassical buildings, plus a sprinkling of more recent additions. Here you will find the **Drinking Hall**, where the highly esteemed local mineral water, Donat Mg, surges directly from a spring. The hall can be accessed through the Rogaška Medical Center.

NOTES

Rogaška Slatina's wealth is built on its mineral water, Donat Mg, on sale throughout Slovenia and exported abroad. Loaded with magnesium, it is said to treat metabolic problems such as obesity, constipation, heartburn and high glucose levels, as well as stress-related diseases and high blood pressure.

For a thorough pampering, the place to go is the **Lotus Health and Beauty Center** (www.rogaska.si/en/grand-hotel-sava-superior) in the *Grand Hotel Sava*. Reservations are necessary for massage, hydrotherapy and beauty treatments. **The Rogaška Riviera complex** (Zdraviliški trg 12; charge; www.rogaska-resort.com) has thermal pools; Turkish, Finnish and infrared saunas; and a solarium; plus it also offers massages.

Rogaška Slatina is known for its crystal glass. Visitors can view and buy glass items from the Rogaška Glassworks' **Tempel** shop at Zdraviliški trg 22, on the main square. In homage to the town's glassmaking industry, there's also a huge **Crystal Tower** (Stolp Kristal; Tržaški Hrib 4; charge; www.stolp-kristal.si): at 106 metres (348ft), it's Slovenia's tallest building, and the viewing platform at the top is designed to resemble local glassworks.

Maribor

Slovenia's second-largest city, **Maribor**, is strung along the left bank of the River Drava, 126km (79 miles) northeast of Ljubljana. Its origins can be traced to the twelfth century, when a fortress (no longer in existence) was built on Piramida Hill to protect the region against the Magyars. A market grew up outside the castle walls, and town status was granted in 1254. Maribor became an important trading centre, with wine and timber transported on the River Drava by raft. In 1846, when railways linked the city first with Vienna and then with Ljubljana, Maribor won its long-standing rivalry with neighbouring Ptuj (see page 76). While the city is more geared towards business travellers than tourists, the old town – an attractive, well-preserved cluster of coloured Baroque facades and steep terracotta tile roofs – is ripe for exploring.

Maribor's most prominent sight is the handsome fifteenth-century **City Castle** (Mestni grad), which houses the **Maribor Regional Museum** (Pokrajinski muzej Maribor; charge; www.museum-mb.si). The ornate interior contains a horde of paintings and sculptures, regional costumes, objects representing various guilds, wine-making tools, and archaeological finds.

Close by, at Trg svobode 3, the impressive **Vinag Wine Cellars** (open to the public for wine tasting, reservations necessary; https://vinag1847.si) are among the largest in Central Europe. Around 2.5km (1.5 miles) of tunnels store 5.5 million litres (1.2 million gallons) of wine, mainly whites, including the esteemed Plenina Royal, a sparkling wine made by the traditional champagne process.

On the southern edge of the old town, close to the river, the **Main Square** (Glavni trg) is arranged around the ornate **Plague Pillar** (Kuž no znamenje), which commemorates a plague that killed one-third of the population between 1680 and 1681. The square's most prominent building is

The rooftops of Maribor

the grey-and-white sixteenth-century **Town Hall** (Rotovž). West of the Main Square, the colourful **Vodnik Square** (Vodnikov trg) holds the town's open-air market.

Along the southern edge of the old town is the **River Drava**, a tributary of the Danube. Here, Lent is a waterside promenade beside the former port area, where boats sailing from Austria to the Black Sea were once obliged to stop for one night and pay port tax. Today, stages are set up in summer along the riverfront for the spectacular Lent Festival (see page 105). Giving onto the river, at Vojašniška 8, **Stara trta** is a 400-year-old grapevine that has earned Maribor a place in the *Guinness Book of Records* as the world's oldest continually producing vine.

Out of town, **Maribor Island** (Mariborski otok) is a popular summer bathing spot. Lying 5km (3 miles) west of the old town, it can be reached on foot or by bike along the riverside promenade. The island is connected by a bridge and has two outdoor pools.

The hills of **Maribor Pohorje** (www.visitpohorje.si), 7km (4 miles) southwest of Maribor and accessible by cable car, are home to one of Slovenia's largest winter ski resorts, as well as offering hiking and mountain-biking opportunities. Here, the **Bike Park Pohorje** (charge; www.visitpohorje.si/en/bike-park) challenges cycling enthusiasts with a 4km (2.5-mile) downhill run.

Ptuj

The flat fertile flood plain of the River Drava separates Maribor from **Ptuj** ⓳, 25km (15 miles) away. Commanding a hilltop position above the plain, Ptuj was founded by the Romans in the first century AD as Poetovio and had 40,000 inhabitants. In 450 it was plundered by the Huns and in the sixth century the ancient city was occupied by the Avars. It passed into the Frankish Empire in the late eighth century, then coming under the Archbishopric of Salzburg, before falling under the Habsburgs in 1555. When neighbouring Maribor was linked by railway to Vienna in the late nineteenth century, Ptuj slid into relative decline. Today, the old town, a tangle of cobbled streets lined with Gothic and Baroque buildings and crowned by a hilltop castle, is known throughout Slovenia for its *Kurentovanje* carnival celebrations.

To learn more about Ptuj's ancient past, visit the former **Dominican Monastery** (Dominikanski samostan; charge; www.dominikanskisamostan.si) on Muzejski trg, where a small archaeological collection includes fragments from three Roman shrines to Mithras, and collections of coins and gems.

Roman relics aside, Ptuj's most impressive sight has to be **Ptuj Castle** (Grad Ptuj), poised on a hill above town and centring on an elegant Baroque courtyard. The castle dates from the twelfth

The cobbled streets of Ptuj, a town known for its carnival

KURENTOVANJE

Carnival celebrations in Ptuj, known as *Kurentovanje*, take place in the ten days leading up to Shrove Tuesday. This raucous street party involves local men dressing up as *Kurent* (or Korant), a god of hedonism. These *kurenti* are clad in sheepskin cloaks with cowbells hung around their waists, and wear terrifying masks with beaky noses, large white teeth and protruding bright-red tongues. The men rampage through the streets, from house to house, making a terrible din with their bells. The tradition is thought to hark back to pagan fertility rites: the *kurenti* are supposed to chase out the winter and welcome in the spring.

century, though its present appearance is the result of alterations carried out between the fifteenth and eighteenth centuries. Today it houses the highly enjoyable **Ptuj Regional Museum** (Pokrajinski muzej Ptuj; charge; www.pmpo.si), displaying a fine collection of musical instruments, period furniture and traditional *Kurentovanje* (carnival) costumes.

Those who enjoy a drop of fine wine should also arrange a visit to the **Wine Cellars** (Vinska klet; Vinarski trg 1; www.ptujska-klet.si; book at least a day in advance). The standard tour includes a look round the vast cellars, a film about winemaking in the region, and a wine-tasting session.

Wine roads around Ptuj

The grape-growing Haloze Hills lie south of Ptuj, close to the border with Croatia. The **Haloze Hills Wine Road** begins at **Borl Castle**, overlooking the River Drava around 11km (7 miles) southeast of Ptuj. The region produces some of Slovenia's best white wines, and along the route there are several vineyards and wine cellars open to the public.

First stop in the Haloze Hills is the village of **Ptujska Gora**, 12km (8 miles) southwest of Ptuj beneath the fifteenth-century **Church**

of the Virgin Mary (Cerkev svete Marije), a popular pilgrimage site attracting 60,000 visitors annually and offering fine views over the River Drava flood plain.

The **Jeruzalem–Ljutomer Wine Road** is tucked into the folds of the undulating hills northeast of Ptuj, running 18km (11 miles) from Ljutomer to **Ormož**. It passes through the hilltop village of **Jeruzalem**, named by the Teutonic Knights who lived here in the twelfth century.

Murska Sobota

Pomurje means 'across the Mura', and it is indeed on the far side of the River Mura, close to the Hungarian border. The region is

Flamboyant carnival masks in Ptuj help the kurenti banish away the winter

characterised by flat, fertile fields and small farming villages, and there is a sizeable Hungarian minority.

Pomurje's chief urban centre is **Murska Sobota**, on the River Ledava. For insight into local life, visit the **Pomurje Museum** (Pomurski muzej; charge; www.pomurski-muzej.si) in an eighteenth-century mansion in the City Park (Mestni Park), where there is an award-winning exhibition.

Moravske Toplice

Another of Slovenia's sophisticated spas, **Moravske Toplice** sits 8km (5 miles) northeast of Murska Sobota. Here, the vast, modern **Terme 3000 –Moravske Toplice** (charge; www.sava-hotels-resorts.com/sl/terme-3000) is an aquatic wonderland, comprising 22 indoor and outdoor pools with geysers, waterfalls, water massage therapies, upstream swimming facilities and hot tubs. There is a diving pool with a hair-raising 22m (72ft) -high platform, plus Turkish and Finnish saunas.

The Thermalium Wellness Centre, with 'black' thermal water, is said to relax and replenish body and soul, improve circulation and reduce nervous agitation.

On the edge of the resort lie the greens of the 18-hole Livada Golf Course (see page 98). The flat, rural terrain makes the area ideal for cycling; the Bike Center at Kranjčeva 8 has bicycles for hire and can also arrange rafting trips on the River Mura.

Southeast

Highlights

- **Stična Monastery**, see page 82
- **Novo mesto**, see page 82
- **Dolenjske Toplice**, see page 84
- **Otočec**, see page 85
- **Pleterje Monastery**, see page 85

- **Kostanjevica na Krki**, see page 86
- **Brežice**, see page 87
- **Bizeljsko**, see page 88
- **Čatež**, see page 88
- **Mokrice Castle**, see page 89

Many visitors pass through the southeast corner of Slovenia en route from Ljubljana to Zagreb in Croatia without stopping along the way. However, this is to overlook a number of small but charming spa towns, watersports on the River Krka, and a string of impressive monasteries, castles and wine cellars open to the public for tastings and tours.

Stična Monastery

Stična Monastery

Stična Monastery ⓴ (Samostan Stična; charge; www.sticna.eu) is tucked away among green meadows close to Ivančna Gorica, 32km (22 miles) from Ljubljana on the A2. Founded by the Cistercians in 1135, Stična is the oldest monastery in Slovenia. In the fifteenth century it was fortified with high walls against Turkish attack, and became the region's main religious, economic, educational and cultural centre. In 1784 it was closed by the Habsburgs, who believed the monasteries had become too powerful, but it reopened in 1898. Today a dozen monks are in residence.

Tours begin with an audiovisual presentation, then pass through the **Slovenian Museum of Christianity** (Muzej krščanstva na Slovenskem), displaying religious paintings, icons, manuscripts, and processional crosses and chalices, as well as objects related to the monks' work, such as bookbinding and farming. Visitors are also shown the Baroque **monastery church** and the thirteenth-century Gothic vaulted cloisters. The tour ends with a peek inside the monastery shop, which sells herbal teas, tinctures and ointments prepared to recipes devised by the late Father Simon Ašič, plus wine and honey made by the monks, and religious souvenirs.

Novo mesto

Southeast Slovenia's largest town and cultural centre of the Dolenjska region is **Novo mesto**, around 55km (34 miles) east of Ljubljana on the A2. In medieval times it was a market town and trading centre, and today it is an important industrial zone and home to the pharmaceutical company Krka. The old town is nestled in a meander on the left bank of the River Krka, accessed by three bridges.

Dolenjska Museum (Dolenjski muzej; Muzejska ulica 7; charge; www.dolenjskimuzej.si), at Muzejska 7, has a highly regarded archaeological collection with Iron and Bronze Age finds, notably *situlae* – ornately decorated bronze urns found in burial sites nearby. There are cultural history, recent history and ethnological collections, and a permanent collection of art from the seventeenth to twentieth centuries – the standout is a miniature three-sectioned portable altar from 1652.

Café life centres on **Main Square** (Glavni trg), a long cobbled piazza, more a street than a square, flanked by sixteenth-century vaulted arcades, which originally housed craft workshops and merchants' stores.

Located just off the south end of Main Square, near the river, the **Božidar Jakac House** (Jakčev dom; charge; www.dolenjskimuzej.si) exhibits sketches and paintings by distinguished local artist

A Dolenjska Museum exhibit about Partisans in World War II

Božidar Jakac (1899–1989). The ground and first floors are devoted to pictures of the region's landscape and inhabitants, while the second floor is filled with paintings from the artist's journeys in Europe and America.

Also worth a look is the **Chapter Church of St Nicholas** (Cerkev svetega Nikolaja), which dates from the fourteenth century and is Novo mesto's oldest surviving building. A highlight is a fine painting of St Nicholas by the renowned Venetian artist Tintoretto (1518–94).

Dolenjske Toplice

The small Austro-Hungarian-style spa town of **Dolenjske Toplice**, 12km (8 miles) southwest of Novo mesto, is home to the large, modern **Balnea Wellness Centre**, with indoor and outdoor pools (charge; www.terme-krka.com), waterfalls and geysers, a sophisticated range of relaxing saunas, plus beauty treatments and massage. For those who prefer adventure sports, there is the chance to raft, kayak or canoe on the River Krka (see page 94).

Otočec Castle

Otočec

The impressive Gothic-Renaissance **Otočec Castle** (Grad Otočec), 7km (4 miles) east of Novo mesto, has been refurbished and now houses the *Hotel Grad Otočec*. Built with four towers, it lies on an island on the River Krka, reached by a wooden bridge. Although it is not open to the public, non-residents are welcome in the upmarket restaurant and café. Otočec Golf Course (see page 98) and the Equestrian School Sport Centre Češča Vas are both close to the castle.

Pleterje Monastery

In a peaceful valley close to the small village of Šentjernej, some 20km (12.5 miles) east of Otočec, is **Pleterje Monastery** ㉑ (Samostan Pleterje; www.kartuzija-pleterje.si). Hidden amid dense woodland and vineyards, the monastery was founded in the fifteenth century. It was fortified against the Turks, only to be lost by the Carthusians in 1593. It was repurchased and reopened in 1904, and is home to about a dozen Carthusian monks. As the Carthusians value silence and solitude, most of Pleterje is closed to visitors. However, it is possible to view the magnificent fifteenth-century Gothic **Church of the Holy Trinity** (Cerkev svete Trojice; daily) and watch a short film about the way the monks live – they practise collective labour, solitary contemplation and abstain from meat.

The monastery also owns a fine collection of old master paintings, but these are now displayed in the Božidar Jakac Gallery in Kostanjevica na Krki (see page 86).

A shop (https://pleter.si) next to the church sells goods produced by the monks, such as wine, honey, potent local spirits – including *viljamovka*, with a whole pear inside the bottle, and *slivovka* made from plums – as well as propolis, mead (honey wine) and beeswax candles. Visitors can also walk the 4km (2.5-mile) **Pleterje Way**, following a marked path – look out for a blue circle and a yellow cross – around the perimeter of the complex, which the monks do on their weekly outing when they are allowed to break their vow of silence.

In the woods, close to the entrance to the monastery, stands the **Pleterje Open-Air Museum** (Muzej na prostem Pleterje; tel: 04-163 91 91; open by appointment). This reconstruction of a nineteenth-century traditional farm includes a wooden, thatch-roof farmhouse with period furniture, a cluster of wooden outbuildings, a potter's workshop, and a stone well. There is a small souvenir shop, and the complex puts on occasional demonstrations of local crafts.

Kostanjevica na Krki

On an island in a deep curve in the River Krka, accessed via two bridges, is the tiny town of **Kostanjevica na Krki**. Some 6km (4 miles) east of Šentjernej, it dates from the eleventh century and has been designated a cultural monument. With just two main streets and a couple of small Gothic churches, it makes an unusual and photogenic destination.

On the southwest of the village at Grajska 45, a disused thirteenth-century Cistercian monastery now shelters the **Božidar Jakac Art Museum** (Galerija Božidar Jakac; charge; www.galerija-bj.si). The collection displays paintings by twentieth-century Slovenian artists, including several fine pastels and oils by Božidar Jakac, who founded the gallery in 1974 and was

Pleterje Monastery

one of the initiators of the Ljubljana Academy of Fine Arts.

There is also a permanent exhibition of 44 paintings by French, Flemish, Italian and German Old Masters belonging to the Pleterje Monastery. In the landscaped grounds, a scattering of wooden sculptures from the international open-air sculpture symposium Forma Viva are on display.

Self-portrait by local artist Božidar Jakac (1899–1989)

Brežice

The picturesque little town of **Brežice** lies 15km (10 miles) east of Kostanjevica na Krki at the point where the River Krka flows into the River Sava. It is well worth a stop to visit the sixteenth-century Renaissance **Brežice Castle** housing the excellent **Brežice Posavski Museum** (Posavski muzej Brežice; charge; www.pmb.si).

The highlight is the Knights' Hall, decorated with exceptional Baroque frescos that create optical illusions. But the museum itself is also interesting, tracing the region's history from the earliest Roman and Celtic settlers to World War II. Each summer the Knights' Hall and the castle courtyard host the Seviqc Brežice Festival of Early Music (mid-June to mid-Aug; www.seviqc.si/about-festival.html), with ancient and Baroque music.

The **Brežice Bicycle Trail**, which begins and ends in Brežice, is a 97km (61-mile) -long round trip with ten checkpoints of either natural or cultural interest, including the spa town of Čatež and the winemaking village of Bizeljsko, 19km (12 miles) northeast of the town.

Bizeljsko

Close to the Croatian border, **Bizeljsko** is known for its unusual *repnice* wine cellars. These underground chambers were originally dug for storing turnips (*repa* means turnip in Slovenian), but their constant low temperatures and humidity also make them perfect for maturing wine, which is what they are mainly used for today. **Vino Graben** (Kumrovška 6; tel: 07-495 10 59) offers tastings and the chance to visit *repnice* cellars.

The Vino Graben order book includes such elite customers as former US president Bill Clinton and several important European royal families.

Čatež

Slovenia's largest natural health resort, **Čatež** (www.terme-catez.si) is 24km (15 miles) east of Novo mesto on the A2, and just 3km (2 miles) southeast of Brežice. Built over underground thermal springs, Čatež was founded in the 1920s, but only really developed into a serious spa resort in the 1960s.

Today it has a selection of modern hotels and receives some 640,000 visitors annually, some of whom come for health treatments and to relax and recharge.

The **Thermal Riviera** is a vast, ultramodern complex consisting of the **Summer Thermal Riviera**, a huge open-air water park comprising seven thermal pools (average temperature 30°C/86°F) fitted with wave machines, waterfalls and slides; plus the indoor **Winter Thermal Riviera**, with yet more pools hosting slides, wave machines, water-massage machines and whirlpools. Another attraction is the large **Sauna Park**, offering a whopping eight different kinds of sauna.

Mokrice Castle

The Renaissance **Mokrice Castle**, located around 8km (5 miles) southeast of Čatež, has been refurbished to accommodate the somewhat imposing but classy *Mokrice Castle Golf Hotel*. Tucked away among rolling parkland and pockets of forest, it is approached over a moat with a drawbridge, and the interior is carefully furnished with period antiques. Although it is not open to the public, non-residents are welcome to book a table to dine in the upmarket restaurant.

There is also an 18-hole golf course (see page 98) in scenic surrounds, and the hotel offers special accommodation packages for golfers.

Čatež, Slovenia's largest health resort

The mountain scenery is glorious for skiing

Things to do

Soaring mountains, broad lakes and crashing rivers make Slovenia a great place to explore nature and get active outdoors. From skiing in winter to hiking and biking in summer, the mountains are a natural playground for sporty types. That's not to say Slovenia is lacking in culture and nightlife; most of the large cities and towns have a thriving scene. Ljubljana, of course, leads the charge with its bars, clubs and music venues, but you'll find art riches and after-dark hangouts in the likes of Maribor, Koper and on the Adriatic coast too. Plus the festival calendar is jam-packed throughout the year for those keen to immerse themselves in local traditions and celebrations

Outdoor activities

In winter, the mountains offer splendid opportunities for skiing, while at other times of the year the hundreds of well-marked hiking trails are extremely popular, as are the country's cycling routes, particularly in Triglav National Park. If your tastes are more water-based, the multitude of rafting, kayaking and canoeing destinations will – literally – float your boat.

Skiing

Skiing is the Slovenes' favourite sport. There are both downhill pistes and cross-country trails, with snow from early December to late March, and slopes suitable for everyone from experienced skiers to novices and children. Kranjska Gora is the main destination, hosting several major annual skiing World Cup competitions, including the Men's Vitranc Cup (https://pokal-vitranc.com); the Audi FIS Alpine Skiing Women's World Cup (https://kranjskagora-worldcup.com); and ski jumping at nearby Planica (www.planica.si).

There are numerous ski resorts across the country; some of the best are listed below. SkiPass tickets are available, which allow you

NOTES

The top area for hiking is Triglav National Park. Its centrepiece is Mount Triglav (2864 metres/9396ft), the country's highest peak. National tradition has it that Slovenes are not truly Slovenian until they have conquered the mountain's summit. The most popular base for hikers is Bohinj, not least because it offers the best starting point for climbing Mount Triglav, via Ukanc.

to use all Slovenian resorts, offering very good value if you're planning a longer trip.

Kranjska Gora (www.kranjska-gora.si), the largest and most popular resort, lies on the edge of Triglav National Park in the northwest. Excellent for beginners and early intermediates, it is popular with families.

Pohorje (www.visitpohorje.si), the second-largest resort, is located just outside Maribor. Its 10km (6-mile) night-time lit ski slope is the longest in Europe.

Rogla (www.rogla.eu) is a resort with good skiing for all levels. It's particularly good for families as it has plenty of slopes for beginners.

Just outside **Bovec** (www.boveckanin.si), the Kanin Ski Centre is the highest (altitude 2300 metres/7550ft), and consequently has the longest season.

Vogel (www.vogel.si), reached via cable car from Ukanc, is one of the country's largest, and, thanks to its location above Lake Bohinj, has stunning scenery.

Krvavec (www.rtc-krvavec.si), near Kranj and Ljubljana, is popular with day-trippers from the capital. There is little accommodation in the ski area so most stay in the valley.

Hiking

Hiking comes a close second to skiing as the Slovenes' top activity. There are over 7000km (4500 miles) of walking trails, marked at intervals with a white circle in a red circle, usually painted on rocks. There are also 178 mountain huts and shelters, managed by the Alpine Association of Slovenia (www.pzs.si), offering basic overnight accommodation. The most iconic hike is the ascent of Mount Triglav – usually a two-day outing – and there are several other outstanding (and challenging) multi-day treks, including the 270km (168 miles) Juliana Trail, which largely keeps to the valley floors, allowing you to see the mighty Alps without needing to scale them, and the Slovenian Mountain Trail, which runs all the way from Maribor to Ankaran near Koper, taking in 21 mountain peaks.

If all that sounds a bit intense, fortunately there are hundreds of single- or half-day hikes through stunning scenery. Gorges such as Vintgar, Tolmin and Mostnica are delightful short walks, and you

Triglav Lake Hut, Triglav National Park

can also enjoy great views from circuits around Lake Bled and Lake Bohinj. The Peč Tromeja climb is particularly enjoyable – a steep ascent to a summit that marks the border between three countries: Slovenia, Italy and Austria.

Most hikes can be undertaken on a self-guided basis, but there are several companies that organise guided treks. Climb Triglav (https://climbtriglav.com) is one well-regarded option; its focus is on the ascent of Triglav but also offers a couple of other two- to three-day treks.

Cycling

Slovenia is one of Europe's top mountain-biking destinations, and many visitors come here specifically to cycle through Triglav National Park and the Soča Valley. The top trails are those in the Julian Alps in the northwest of the country, though there are routes all over Slovenia, catering for mountain biking or on-road cycling. Particular highlights include the challenging ascent from Kranjska Gora to the Mangart Saddle, involving an altitude change of 1600 metres and 17 hairpin bends to negotiate. Cycling over the Vršič Pass between Kranjska Gora and Bovec is another top choice. For a real challenge, you could take on the Slovenian Bicycle Touring Path, a 1800km (1120 mile) route that takes in virtually the entire country. From end to end, it's a 35-day adventure.

Several UK-based cycling-focused tour companies offer all-inclusive cycling holidays in Slovenia, including **Skedaddle** (www.skedaddle.com/uk) and **Freedom Treks** (www.freedomtreks.co.uk).

Watersports

A series of falls and rapids on the **River Soča** makes it one of the most beautiful and challenging rivers in Europe for rafting, kayaking, canoeing and hydrospeed. The main bases are Bovec and Kobarid. In addition, the **River Krka**, in the southeast, makes a fine venue for watersports, albeit on slightly tamer waters. The Soča

Valley is also the top destination for canyoning, and the main base is at Bovec. Routes range from beginner to extreme canyoning, which includes abseiling.

Numerous companies cater for thrill-seekers hoping to enjoy such activities. Some of the best include:

3glav Adventures Ljubljanska 1, Bled, www.3glav.com.

Alpe Sport Vančar Trg golobarskih žrtev 20, Bovec, www.bovecsport.com.

Alpinsport Ribčev Laz 53, Bohinj, www.alpinsport.si.

Bovec Rafting Team Bovec, www.bovec-rafting-team.com.

Soča Rafting Trg golobarskih žrtev 14, Bovec, www.socarafting.si.

X Point Trg svobode 6, Kobarid, www.xpoint.si.

Cyclists at Triglav National Park

Fishing

The top places for fishing are the **River Soča** (where Kobarid makes a perfect base), **Lake Bohinj** in Triglav National Park, and the **River Krka** in the southeast. In the **Soča and Krka**, the likely catches are marble trout and grayling, while **Bohinj** is home to numerous species of trout, as well as chub, charr and burbot.

Other excellent fishing spots include the **River Sava**, where you're likely to land Danube salmon, and **Lake Šmartinsko**, near Celje, which is rich in carp. The **Fisheries Research Institute of Slovenia** (Spodnje Gameljne 61a, Ljubljana; www.zzrs.si) provides

EXTREME SPORTS ACHIEVEMENTS

In contrast to the other countries of former Yugoslavia, which have achieved international success in team sports such as football and basketball, Slovenes have always excelled in individual sports. In 2000, Davo Karničar became the first man to ski the whole way down Mount Everest, from an altitude of 8850 metres (29,035ft) down to the base camp at 5340 metres (17,500ft), in just under 5hr. He subsequently went on to ski down the highest mountains on the other six continents, becoming the first person to do so after his descent of Vincent Massif, Antarctica, in 2006.

Meanwhile, in 2000, professional marathon swimmer Martin Strel swam the entire 3004km (1867-mile) length of the River Danube in 58 days. In 2001, again on the Danube, he set a new world record for non-stop swimming, covering 500km (313 miles) in 84hr 10min, and in 2002, he swam 3797km (2360 miles) of the Mississippi in North America.

In the cycling field, Marko Baloh is the one to watch: in 2002 he set a new world record by cycling continuously for 12hr, clocking up 452km (281 miles) at the Novo mesto Velodrome. In 2010 he broke his own record with an astonishing non-stop 24hr cycle at the Montichiari Velodrome in Brescia, Italy pedalling a distance of 903km (561 miles).

All three achievements have earned Slovenia places in the *Guinness Book of Records*.

information about fishing, seasons and permits.

Sailing

Slovenia is a perfect launching place for sailing down the Adriatic. The country has three well-equipped boating marinas: Portorož, Koper and Izola, each of which has been awarded a European Blue Flag for safety, cleanliness and respect for the natural environment. There are several charter companies offering boats for hire, and if you do not have a sailing licence, they will also provide a skipper.

Rafting on the Soča

Some reliable options include **Portorož Marina**, Cesta solinarjev 8, www.marinap.si; **Izola Marina**, Tomažičeva 4a, https://marinaup.com and **Koper Marina**, Kopališko nabrežje 5, www.marina-koper.si.

Golf

There are numerous excellent golf courses in Slovenia, all in scenic surrounds. The oldest and the most beautiful is the **Royal Bled Golf Club** (www.royalbled.com) near Lake Bled: the nine-hole Lake Course was laid out in 1938, and the splendid 18-hole King's Course was designed by Donald Harradine in 1972. Reservations are needed at least three days in advance. Some of the country's other top golf courses include:

Golf is popular in Slovenia

Lipica (www.lipica.org/en/golf), a nine-hole course set in the southwest's unique karst limestone scenery.

Golf Course Arboretum (www.golfarboretum.si), an 18-hole course adjoining Volčji Potok Arboretum, near Kamnik.

Golf Grad Mokrice (www.terme-catez.si), an 18-hole course laid out in parkland and woods close to Mokrice Castle in the Krka Valley.

Ptuj (www.golfklubptuj.si), an 18-hole course noted for its water hazards, including two lakes.

Livada (www.sava-hotels-resorts.com), an 18-hole course – including Slovenia's longest hole – on the edge of Moravske Toplice spa complex, in the northeast.

Otočec Golf Course (www.golf-otocec.si), an 18-hole course stretching over hilly terrain along the banks of the River Krka near Otočec Castle.

Zlati Grič (www.golfzlatigric.si), a nine-hole course among picturesque vineyards in Slovenske Konjice, between Celje and Maribor.

Horse riding

The beautiful unspoiled countryside is ideal for trekking. There are several highly professional equestrian schools, the best-known being the famous **Lipica Stud Farm** (www.lipica.org). It offers individual lessons, plus hacking in guided groups. **Mrcina Ranč** (www.ranc-mrcina.com), in Studor, near Lake Bohinj, has Icelandic ponies and Lipizzaner horses for trekking. **Pristava Lepena** (www.pristava-lepena.com), in the Lepena Valley in Triglav National Park, keeps a stable of Lipizzaner horses and gives lessons at all levels, plus group trekking.

Spas

Under Austro-Hungarian rule, spa towns became fashionable with the aristocracy. There are fourteen spas today, all of which come under the umbrella of the Slovenian Spas Community (https://slovenia-spa.si) and are recognised by the Slovenian national health system.

However, they now offer much more than just medical treatment and convalescence, and many have sophisticated wellness centres and hydrotherapy parks. The majority of the country's spas can be found in the northeast, and offer experiences ranging from natural remedies to luxurious pampering.

Shopping

You'll find plenty of the usual European high-street names in Slovenia, particularly in Ljubljana. However, for many foreign

BEACHES AND BATHING

With just 47km (26 miles) of coast, Slovenian beaches get very crowded in the summer, and many Slovenes prefer to venture to neighbouring Croatia. Visitors should note that, in many cases, coastal hotels claiming to have a beach in fact offer no more than a concrete platform affording easy access into the water. The most organised beach is in Portorož, where a strip of imported sand is lined with sunloungers and umbrellas. The best natural beaches can be found between Piran and Fiesa, and at Strunjan, just north of Fiesa. Strunjan has an area reserved for nudists. The water temperature is ideal for swimming from June to mid-October, though hardy types might manage both earlier and later.

visitors the most enjoyable shopping experience remains a visit to the open-air markets, where besides fresh fruit and vegetables, some of the best purchases are locally produced honey, and dried herbs for cooking and preparing tea. The largest and most colourful markets are found in Ljubljana and Maribor.

In Ljubljana you can find upmarket boutiques and antique shops on Town Square (Mestni trg) and Old Square (Stari trg) in the old town, while high-street clothing stores can be found on the pedestrianised Čopova near the Triple Bridge.

In Maribor the main shopping streets are Gosposka and Koper Čeviljarska, both in the old town. BTC City, a large mall, lies 3km (1.5 miles) northeast of Ljubljana city centre and has more than four hundred shops, a microbrewery, a multiplex cinema, a sports hall and the Atlantis Waterpark.

Open-air markets are popular in Slovenia

Gifts you might wish to bring back from Slovenia include the **herbal teas** and **honey** made by monks from Stična Monastery, *viljamovka* and *slivovka* (both **fruit-based spirits**) from Pleterje Monastery, or traditional *medica* honey liqueur, which is sold at numerous stalls in the Ljubljana open-air market. Non-edible souvenirs include **handmade lace** from Idrija and **crystal glass** from Rogaška Slatina; if you're not travelling to either town, both products can be found easily in Ljubljana, the former at Galerija Idrijske Čipke (Mestni trg 17) and the latter at the Rogaska Crystal store (Mestni trg 22). For quality outdoor sports equipment, try Elan **skis** and **snowboards**, and Planika **hiking boots**. Finally, it's almost impossible to leave Ljubljana without picking up a piece of dragon-themed memorabilia: the Dragon Shop at Ciril-Metodov trg 10 offers the widest selection.

Local **wines** can be purchased directly from vineyards and wine cellars. The Tourist Board has devised a series of countrywide *vinske ceste* (wine roads), leading directly to cellars open to the public. Wine-tasting sessions normally include a range of the producer's bottles, starting with dry (*suho*) varieties and progressing to the sweet (*sladko*) ones, accompanied by salty nibbles such as *pršut* (air-dried ham), cheese and home-made bread. It is advisable to telephone the cellars at least one day in advance to confirm the time of your visit. Recommended cellars include **Vinska klet**, Vinarski trg 1, Ptuj (www.ptujska-klet.si); **Vinag Wine Cellars**, Trg svobode 3, Maribor (https://vinag1847.si); and **Klet Brda wine cellars**, Zadružna cesta 9, Dobrovo (www.klet-brda.si).

Nightlife

A large student population guarantees an animated nightlife in Ljubljana. The most popular bars and cafés grace the city centre, with outdoor tables lining the riverside promenade of Cankarjevo nabrežje, plus an increasing number of lounge and cocktail bars on Town Square (Mestni trg) and Old Square (Stari trg) in the old town.

The most popular include **Captain's Cabin** (Ključavničarska 5, http://captains-cabin.si), a see-and-be-seen bar with over a hundred cocktails; **Premier Pub** (Petkovškovo 17, https://tinyurl.com/premierpubljubljana), one of the most lively hangouts in town; **Vinoteka Movia** (Mestni trg 2, www.movia.si), a small, sophisticated, candlelit bar with an excellent wine list; **Silk**

A lively pavement culture

and Fizz (Krojaška 3), for imaginative and perfectly mixed cocktails; and **Makalonca** (Hribarjevo nabrežje 19), where DJs play house, funk and soul indoors, and outside candlelit tables overlook the river in summer.

Nightclubs are relatively thin on the ground, but include **Circus Klub** (Trg mladinskih brigad 7, https://cirkusklub.si), which remains open until 5am on Fridays and Saturdays. The alternative crowd meet at the student-run **Klub K4** (Kersnikova 4, https://klub-k4.si) and **Metelkova** (Metelkova, www.metelkovamesto.org), a squat moonlighting as an arts centre. The Metelkova district is also home to **Tiffany** (Masarykova 24, www.kulturnicenterq.org), one of the country's top gay bars, which runs excellent club nights on Fridays.

In **Maribor**, **Patrick's Pub** (Poštna 10, between Glavni trg and Slomski trg, www.facebook.com/patricks.maribor) is a cosy Irish pub that stays open until 2am on Friday and Saturday; **Klub KGB** (Vojašniški trg 5) is a great place to catch live alternative music; and **Papagayo Cocktail Bar** (Gosposka 6, www.facebook.com/PapagayoMaribor) is a trendy lounge bar that turns into a popular nightclub at weekends.

Slovenia's Adriatic coast was once known for a hedonistic vibe, particularly **Izola**, but since the mid-2010s the clubbing scene has dwindled. Even so, during the summer, late-night revellers still head for **Portorož**, where clubs include **Alaya** (Obala 14a, www.alaya.si) and **Pergola** (Obala 20, www.facebook.com/PergolaPrestigeClub). If a quiet drink is more your thing, try the café at **Hotel Piran** (Stjenkova 1) overlooking the harbour in Piran, or **Loggia Café** (Titov trg 1) inside the seventeenth-century Venetian loggia on the main square in Koper.

Culture

In **Ljubljana**, the Philharmonic Hall (Slovenska Filharmonija; Kongresni trg 10, www.filharmonija.si) is the top venue for classical music concerts, while SNG Opera in Balet Ljubljana (Župančičeva 1, www.opera.si) hosts opera and ballet. Cankarjev dom (Prešernova 10, www.cd-cc.si) is a multipurpose cultural centre staging concerts of all genres, including classical, opera, pop and jazz, as well as theatre, dance, film and art exhibitions. For arts cinema, the best place in town is Kinoteka (Miklošičeva 28, www.kinoteka.si).

Jazz enthusiasts should check out **Soho** (Vilharjeva 43, www.facebook.com/soholjubljana), where local and international musicians take to the stage, or the **Ljubljana Castle Jazz Club** (www.ljubljanskigrad.si/en/why-to-the-castle/jazz-club-en-us) for performances in the castle grounds.

Although Ljubljana doesn't tend to be on the touring circuit for big-name pop and rock artists, the city still attracts a fairly lively concert scene: check out who's playing at **Orto** (Grablovičeva 1, www.orto-bar.com). You'll also find occasional live concerts and theatrical performances at the student-run nightclub **Klub K4** (Kersnikova 4, https://klub-k4.si).

Beyond the capital, in **Maribor**, the **Slovenian National Theatre**, or SNG (Slovensko narodno gledališče; Slovenska ulica 27, www.sng-mb.si) has theatre and opera, while in **Koper**, the Koper Theatre (Gledališče Koper; Verdijeva 3, www.gledalisce-koper.si) is the top venue for drama on the coast.

Slovenia has a busy festival calendar

Children's activities

Mountain walks and picnics, rowing boats on the lakes, toes-in-the-sand fun on the beaches and poking about in castles and caves should all keep children happy. Attractions that should particularly appeal include a visit to the beautiful white Lipizzaner horses at the **Lipica Stud Farm**, a tour of the **Idrija Mercury Mine**, and a ride aboard a miniature train through the chambers and tunnels of **Postojna Cave**, filled with stalagmites and stalactites. Remember also that many spas have special areas for children, and some have waterparks with wave machines, waterfalls and slides.

Festivals and events

Slovenia's rich cultural heritage is reflected in the country's extensive calendar of festivals and events, which offer an insight into the national character and traditions. Particular highlights on the calendar include Ptuj's *Kurentovanje* (carnival; https://kurentovanje.net), Ljubljana's Summer Festival (www.ljubljanafestival.si), and the Lent Festival (www.festival-lent.si) in Maribor.

January Kranjska Gora holds the Audi FIS Alpine Skiing Women's World Cup.

February *Kurentovanje* (carnival) celebrations in Ptuj take place during the ten days running up to Shrove Tuesday.

March Ski Jumping World Championship held at Planica near Kranjska Gora.
Late May or early June Druga Godba, alternative world music festival in Ljubljana.
May to June Exodos festival of contemporary performing arts held in Ljubljana.
June Lent Festival, two-week event featuring music, dance and theatre on the banks of the River Drava in Maribor.
June (last weekend) Medieval street festival, Škofja Loka.
June to mid-September Ljubljana Summer Festival: open-air music, dance and theatre.
Mid-June to mid-August Seviqc Brežice Festival of Early Music. European musicians play ancient and Baroque pieces at Brežice Castle and other Slovenian cultural heritage sites.
Mid-June Bled International Regatta, world-class rowing on Lake Bled.
Late June Idrija hosts a ten-day Lacemaking Festival (Festival idrijske čipke) with displays and events around town.
Late June to early July Bled International Music Festival, two-week event.
Early July Ljubljana Jazz Festival, three days of world-class jazz.
Mid-July Laško celebrates its beer with the several-day Beer and Flowers festival (Laško Pivo in Cvetje).
August Knights' Tournament at Predjama Castle commemorates medieval chivalry.
Mid-August to mid-September Tartini Festival, Piran, pays homage to the works of the eighteenth-century violinist and composer, Giuseppe Tartini.
Early September Stara Trta, Ceremonial Grape Harvest, Maribor.
Late October Ljubljana Marathon.
11 November Martinovanje (St Martin's Day) celebrates the year's new wine, with festivities all over the country, most notably in Maribor.

Food and drink

Slovenian cuisine, like its history, is a blend of Austro-Hungarian and Venetian influences. Hefty Central European options such as *dunajski zrezek* (wiener schnitzel) and *golaž* (goulash) sit side by side with the more Italian flavours of *pršut* (prosciutto) and *rižota* (risotto). Plus, there's an array of wholesome Slovenian country dishes guaranteed to fill you up, including *klobasa* (sausage) served with *kislo zelje* (sauerkraut), *krvavica* (black pudding) with *žganci* (wheat, buckwheat or corn polenta), or *cmoki* (dumplings).

Given the size of the country, it's not too surprising that there's little regional variation in the dishes on offer, though it goes

Outdoor dining

without saying that seafood is more abundant and more likely to be fresh (not frozen) on the coast, while the best trout is to be found in lakeside or riverside restaurants. You'll find the best selection of restaurants in the cities – Ljubljana, in particular, has an abundance of great places to eat – but even in the smallest villages you're likely to have the option eating in a *gostilna* (tavern). Look out, too, for culinary pop-ups: in Ljubljana, the central market frequently hosts a tremendous food market where you can browse stalls for the best street eats, making an ideal lunch stop.

Ljubljana is full of restaurants

Top 10 things to try

1. Idrijski žlikrofi

The first ever Slovenian dish to be granted Traditional Specialities Guaranteed (TSG) – a hallmark of classic food types, whether in production, preparation or recipes – *idrijski žlikrofi* are traditional small dumplings made of simple pasta dough, which is rolled out and stuffed with cooked potatoes mixed with herbs and spices (such as chives, marjoram, salt, pepper), sautéed onions and sometimes bacon. Moulded to form little 'ears' with hollows in them, *žlikrofi* are then cooked in boiling water. Once ready, the dumplings can be served as an appetiser or as a main dish with

NOTES

Italians are often known to drive over the border into Slovenia for lunch or dinner, a mark of the high quality of the country's restaurants.

lamb or vegetable sauce or coated in breadcrumbs. The traditional *idrijski žlikrofi* should always have a characteristic 'hat' shape and be small enough to eat in a single mouthful.

2. Carniolan sausage

Sausages, considered a snack or a light lunch, come in a variety of forms in Slovenia, yet by far the tastiest type is *kranjska klobasa*. Otherwise known as the Carniolan sausage, it's a Slovene culinary speciality produced using pork, bacon and spices – primarily garlic, salt, saltpetre and black pepper – stuffed into pork intestine. The sausage is then hot-smoked and heat-cured at around 70°C. When ready, it is served whole, warm – most often with sauerkraut or turnips – or cold, with a dollop of mustard, ketchup or horseradish and a slice of bread.

3. Pršut

Pršut is a common form of delicious dry-cured ham, very popular in Slovenia and other Balkan countries, usually served as a cold or hot appetiser (*predjedi – hladne ali tople*). Similar to Italian prosciutto, it's often accompanied by olives, melon or cheese. *Pršut* pairs particularly well with a glass of Kraški Teran, a Slovenian full-bodied red wine. One particular variant to look out for is *Kraški pršut* – hailing from the Karst region – which has a Protected Geographical Indication (PGI) status in the European Union and the UK.

4. Pohorski pisker

Originating from the region of Pohorje in the northeast of Slovenia, *pohorski pisker* is very popular nationally. Especially welcome in the cold winter months, this hearty Slovenian stew is usually made of several meat types – most often beef, lamb and pork – and generously seasoned, typically with a combination of garlic, salt, pepper, cumin and marjoram. Other staple ingredients are mushrooms, barley and potatoes. As there is no set recipe for *pohorski pisker*, additional produce may also be added, including venison and bacon, as well as – depending on the season – carrots, onions, cabbage, beans or chickpeas.

5. Seafood

There are several excellent seafood restaurants in Ljubljana, with daily deliveries of fresh fish from the coast, but to enjoy the very best seafood you'll need to head to one of the seaside towns in the

Idrijski žlikrofi, a Slovene speciality

southwest. Kick off with *hobotnica v solati* (octopus salad) or *školjke* (mussels), followed by fresh fish *na žaru* (barbecued) – favourites include *brancin* (sea bass) and *orada* (gilthead bream).

6. Gibanica

Gibanica, or *Prekmurska gibanica*, is a delicious sweet, layered pastry stuffed with cottage cheese, poppy seeds, walnut and apple, originally hailing from the northeastern Slovenian region of Prekmurje but very popular throughout the entire country. You can occasionally find it served with sour cream, which adds considerably to its richness. The oldest written record of *Prekmurska gibanica* dates back to the 1820s, when it was traditionally served at weddings.

7. Kremšnita

The delicious cream cake known as *kremšnita* is one of the most popular desserts in the country. Traditionally attributed to the Austro-Hungarian court – the word *kremšnita* is derived from the German *Cremeschnitte* (cream slice) – this sweet treat is comprised of vanilla and whipped cream, topped with a layer of flaky pastry. It is difficult to say whether or not there is just one specific type, since each café (*kavarna*) has its own recipe and secret ingredients. It can be found all over Slovenia, though there's a particular concentration of great places to try it in Ljubljana and Bled.

8. Honey

There's a long-standing tradition of apiculture in Slovenia – traced in Radovljica's Beekeeping Museum (see page 44) – which means that the country is among Europe's top honey producers. In 2024's European Honey Contest, Slovenia scooped first prize in a whopping ten out of eleven categories. There are numerous varieties to try, including the very light acacia honey and the rich spruce honey. It can be bought direct from beekeepers across the country, or from marketplaces in the larger towns.

Over 25 million gallons of wine are produced each year

9. Wine

Slovenia produces top-quality wine (*vino*), most of which is consumed within the country and never reaches the export market. Along the coast, be sure to try the white (*belo*) Malvazija, which is an excellent accompaniment to seafood, and the red (*rdeče*) Refošk, which pairs well with meat dishes. In the Karst region, the star is the robust red Teran, which is made from the same grape as Refošk, but here results in a significantly different wine due to the variation in both the soil and the climate. In the northeast, semi-dry and semi-sweet whites predominate, while in the southeast, the favourite tipple is Cviček, a light, sharp, rose-coloured wine, unique to Slovenia, which is produced from a blend of red and white grapes. Unless you order a whole bottle, wine is served and priced by the decilitre (*deci*, one-tenth, pronounced 'de-tsee'). A normal glass contains two *deci*.

10. Beer

The two main breweries in Slovenia are Laško, based in the town of the same name and producer of Zlatorog (named after the mythical chamois), and the Ljubljana-based Union; once separate companies, these are now both owned by Heineken. Both also produce *temno pivo* (literally 'dark beer'), a Guinness-like stout. Evening beer drinking usually takes place in café-bars as well as in the more traditional *pivnica* (pub or beer hall). There has also been a mushrooming of microbreweries throughout the country, which put out an exciting and refreshingly original range of craft beers, including pale ales, IPAs and stouts. Microbreweries to look out for include Pelicon from Ajdovščina and Reservoir Dogs in Nova Gorica.

Enjoying alfresco drinks on a riverside promenade in Ljubljana

Where to eat

To rub shoulders with the locals and experience something close to home cooking, eat at an informal *gostilna* (tavern) or *gostišče* (inn – these offer accommodation as well as food). The better ones are cosy, old-fashioned establishments, with rustic interiors and an informal atmosphere. The menu is usually limited, but the standard of the food is always reliable. At lunchtime many offer a bargain-priced fixed menu (*dnevno kosilo*), consisting of three courses: soup, a main course and a side salad.

Kraški pršut

For the most authentic experience, try a *turistična kmetija* (agrotourism centre), where you are guaranteed top-notch home cooking using fresh, locally produced ingredients. Most serve home-made wine, olive oil, cheese and sausages, along with fresh baked bread, and seasonal specialities such as *špargljі* (asparagus) in spring or *gobe* (mushrooms) and *radič* (radicchio) in autumn. The carefully restored old stone farmhouses set in rural surroundings are often worth the visit in themselves, and some offer overnight accommodation and countryside activities such as horse riding. Note that most agrotourism centres prefer you to telephone at least one day in advance so they can prepare for your arrival.

On a similar note, it is worth looking out for the country's excellent 'Slow Food' establishments. These put an emphasis on old-fashioned recipes prepared from superior local produce. Meals are served at a relaxed pace, generally consisting of eight courses or more, with a different wine to accompany each course.

By and large, restaurants and eateries in smaller towns and villages tend to stick to local cuisine, although no matter where you are, you'll probably be able to source a *pica* (pizza), which often will be on a par with those across the border in Italy. In the larger towns and cities – especially Ljubljana – there's a considerable amount of variation in the cuisines on offer, ranging from Slovenian dishes to international flavours such as Indian, Chinese and Mexican.

Last but not least, grills and snack bars, known as *bife* or *okrepčevalnica*, serve cheap and sometimes rather greasy Balkan favourites such as *pljeskavice* (burgers) and *čevapčiči* (meat

Kremšnita, a traditional sweet treat

croquettes), plus Balkan-style *burek* (filo-pastry pie filled with either cheese or minced meat).

Grilled sea bass with polenta

When to eat

Zajtrk (breakfast) in a hotel is usually a self-service cold buffet. The better ones offer yoghurt, cereal, fruit, meats, cheese, hard-boiled eggs, sausages, bread, butter, jam and honey. If your accommodation does not include breakfast, you can wake up over a cup of coffee in a café, and plenty of places in Ljubljana and other larger towns offer decent menus. For pastries and cakes, track down a *slaščičarna* (cake shop).

Kosilo (lunch) is generally eaten between noon and 2pm. In some of the busier resorts, restaurants operate all afternoon. Alternatively, if you are sightseeing you might prefer to make do with a snack, or if you are hiking you could pack a picnic: stock up on supplies from the local market.

Večerja (dinner) is normally eaten between 7pm and 10pm. However, there are no hard and fast rules: some restaurants along the coast stay open late in summer, while those in the mountains tend to close early all year-round (in Bohinj most are shut by 10pm).

Note that most restaurants are closed one day a week, to give the staff a day off. In working cities such as Ljubljana, this will usually occur on Sunday (when many locals head out of town anyway), while in the resorts it is more likely to be on Monday.

To help you order ...

Waiter/Waitress! **Natakar/Gospodična, prosim!**
Could we have a table? **Ali bi lahko dobili mizo?**
I'd like ... **Rad(a) bi ...**
I'd like to pay. **Rad(a) bi plačal(a).**

bread **kruh**
butter **maslo**
coffee **kava**
fish dishes **ribje jedi**
fruit **sadje**
ice cream **sladoled**
meat dishes **mesne jedi**
mer u **jedilnik**
milk **mleko**
pepper **poper**
potato **krompir**
rice **riž**
salad **solata**
salt **sol**

Traditional potica

soup **juha**
sugar **sladkor**
tea **čaj**
wine **vino**

... and read the menu

bakala cod
burek filo-pastry pie
fazan pheasant
golaž goulash
gos goose
jetra liver
klobasa sausage
krvavica black pudding
ligne squid
medved bear
njoki gnocchi
palačinke pancakes
pivo beer
piščanec chicken
postrvi trout
puran turkey
rižota risotto
salama salami
sir cheese
škampi shrimps
školjke mussels
sladoled ice cream
smetana sour cream
sok fruit juice
srna venison
šunka ham (boiled)
testenine pasta
voda water
zajec rabbit
zavitek strudel
žganci polenta
zrezek cutlet

Slovenian specialities

čevapčiči meat rissoles
hobotnica v solati octopus salad
jota soup with beans, sauerkraut and barley
kranjska klobasa firm, meaty sausage
ocvrti sir cheese fried in breadcrumbs
potica rolled cake with poppy seeds or walnuts
prekmurska gibanica layer cake (cream cheese, walnuts, apple)
pršut air-dried ham, like Italian prosciutto
sarma cabbage rolls with rice and minced meat
štruklji rolled dumpling (savoury or sweet)
žlikrofi speciality from Idrija, similar to ravioli

Places to eat

Each restaurant and café reviewed in this Guide is accompanied by a price category, based on the cost of a three-course meal (or similar) for one, excluding wine:

€€€€ = over 40 euros
€€€ = 25–40 euros
€€ = 10–25 euros
€ = below 10 euros

Ljubljana

Ala Pršuterija Cankarjevo nabrežje 9, www.facebook.com/alaprsuterija. Excellent bar-restaurant on the banks of the Ljubljanica, with a great menu of small plates. It's a particularly good spot to sample *pršut* – the Slovenian take on prosciutto – as well as local cheeses. **€€**

AS Čopova 5a (off Knafljev prehod), www.gostilnaas.si. This outstanding restaurant, considered one of the best in town, is hidden away in a courtyard close to Wolfova ulica. The ambience is old-fashioned, with formal service, crisp white table linen and antique furniture, while the menu is particularly strong on excellent seafood and refined pasta dishes. Reservations recommended. **€€€€**

Julija Stari trg 9, www.julijarestaurant.com. This stylish but informal restaurant lies in the heart of the old town, with an interior decorated with ornate gilded mirrors. The cuisine is creative Mediterranean, with house specialities, including octopus and rocket salad, and risotto with porcini mushrooms. **€€€**

Klobasarna Ciril-Metodov trg 15, www.klobasarna.si. A small and inexpensive haunt in the old town with a short but tasty menu composed mainly of the local *klobasa* (sausage), soup and porridge. **€**

Ljubljanski dvor Dvorni trg 1, https://ljubljanskidvor.si. With a beautiful open-air terrace close to Shoemaker's Bridge, *Ljubljanski dvor* offers a magnificent selection of thin-based pizzas, said by many to be the best in town. **€€**

Odprta Kuhna Pogačarjev trg, www.odprtakuhna.si. In the brighter months, the locals flock to the terrific 'Open Kitchen', a buzzing open-air food market where some of the city's (and Slovenia's) very best restaurants (including *Strelec* and *AS*) serve sample portions of their dishes at cheaper prices. Mid-March to Oct Fri 8am–10pm, weather permitting. **€€**

Pri Škofu Rečna 8, Krakovo, www.facebook.com/gostilnica.priskofu. Much loved by both locals and visitors, this friendly restaurant has a daily changing menu. Expect Slovenian favourites, such as octopus salad, gnocchi, risotto, and buckwheat *štruki* (dumplings), in a colourful, Bohemian setting. **€€**

Špajza Gornji trg 28, tel: 01-425 30 94. A romantic and cosy retreat for dinner in the old town, *Špajza* serves inventive Mediterranean dishes, such as grilled mushrooms with gorgonzola and creamy shrimp risotto, in a series of candlelit rooms on the hill below the castle. **€€€**

Northwest

Bled

Čarman Cesta svobode 37, https://tinyurl.com/carmanbled. A twenty-minute walk along the lakeside from Bled centre brings you to this friendly restaurant, which offers a great menu of local and international dishes. Try to nab an upstairs table for lovely views over the lake. **€€**

Pri Planincu Grajska 8, www.pri-planincu.com. Located above Lake Bled, on the road to the castle, this much-loved restaurant serves up hearty

Slovenian food, such as *klobasa* (sausage), *krvavica* (black pudding) and walnut *štruklji* (dumplings), plus pizza. At lunchtime, locals sit in the front room over beer and the fixed-price menu of the day. **€€**

Vila Prešeren Veslaška promenada 14, https://vilapreseren.com/restavracija. Located in a white villa dating back to 1868, this used to be a holiday retreat for high-ranking officers in the Yugoslav National Army. Today the upmarket lakeside restaurant offers sophisticated dishes such as pasta with smoked salmon and gilt-head bream filled with mushrooms. The dining room is quite formal, and there's a lovely summer terrace with views across the water to the island. **€€€€**

Bohinj

Gostilna Rupa Srednja vas 87, www.gostilna-rupa.si. Five kilometres (3 miles) from Ribčev Laz, this popular inn dishes up substantial portions of home cooking on a terrace with lovely views of the valley and mountains. Specialities include local trout, pork and venison. Occasional live music. **€€€**

Ukanc Ukanc 20, www.restavracija-ukanc.com. At the west end of the lake, on the way to Savica waterfall, *Ukanc* serves up delicious fresh trout, as well as other local favourites with a meaty focus. There are outdoor tables on the terrace in summer. **€€**

Kobarid

Topli Val Trg svobode 1, www.hotelhvala.si. On the ground floor of *Hotel Hvala*, this highly regarded restaurant offers some of the best seafood in the country, with daily deliveries direct from the coast, plus local river fish. Long-standing favourites include creamy prawn soup, shellfish prepared Dalmatian-style in olive oil and garlic, trout in fennel sauce and sea bass baked in a salt crust. The house dessert is *kobariški štruklji* (dumplings with walnut filling). **€€€€**

Kranjska Gora

Gostilna pri Martinu Borovška 61, https://gostilnaprimartinu.si/restavracija. This reliable, old-fashioned inn plates up wholesome Slovenian favourites such as trout, veal, home-made sausages and dumplings. **€€€**

Radovljica

Gostilna Lectar Linhartov trg 2, www.lectar.com. Occupying a sixteenth-century building, *Gostilna Lectar* has been an inn since 1822. It serves local specialities, such as pumpkin soup, buckwheat *štruklji* (dumplings) and apple strudel, in a cosy, rustic dining room with a beamed ceiling and an open fire. In summer there are also tables outdoors in the garden. **€€€**

Southwest

Idrija

Barbara Kosovelova 3, www.gostiscebarbara.si. The best place to try the local speciality, *žlikrofi* (marjoram-spiked potato balls wrapped in pasta), served here in a rich truffle sauce. Main courses include venison and wild boar, followed by a selection of home-made gateaux for dessert. The staff can also arrange cooking and wine-tasting classes. **€€€**

Gostilna pri Škafarju Ulica Svete Barbare 9, www.skafar.si. Fairly plain-looking, but with a decent menu, including *žlikrofi* prepared various ways – perhaps with mushrooms, pork or lamb. Finish with the house speciality, a strawberry and mascarpone mousse topped with glazed chocolate. **€€**

Koper

Caprizza Pristaniška 3, www.grandkoper.com/restaurants. Served in a stylish dining room with views out over the harbour, this is the best place in Koper to come for Italian-style wood-fired pizza. The pavement seating on summer days makes it a delightful place to linger. **€€**

Istrska klet Slavček Župančičeva 39, www.facebook.com/istrskakletslavcek. In the old town, this tiny rustic wine bar rustles up home-made Istrian specialities such as *jota* (bean soup), *pršut* and *ligne* (squid). **€**

Piran

Ivo Gregorčičeva 3, https://gostilna-ivo.com. Of the string of touristy seafood restaurants that lines Piran's coastal promenade, unpretentious *Ivo* is one of the best. Try the grilled squid and barbecued sea bass, or order the fish platter for two. The summer terrace has a fine sea view. **€€€**

Neptun Župančičeva 7, tel: 05-673 41 11. Still one of the best restaurants in town according to locals, tiny *Neptun* serves Italian-inspired dishes such as gnocchi with shrimps and gorgonzola, plus quality fresh fish prepared over charcoal. **€€€€**

Portorož

Ribič Seča, tel: 05-677 07 90. Most of Portorož's restaurants are impersonal establishments attached to hotels lining the seafront promenade. But *Ribič*, 1.5km (1 mile) out of town on the way to the Sečovlje saltpans, has its own garden terrace giving onto the sea. This seafood restaurant serves excellent mussels, shrimps and barbecued fresh fish, plus good local wines. **€€€**

Northeast

Ivanjkovci

Taverna Svetinje 21, https://taverna-kupljen.si. A perfect spot for lunch in the Jeruzalem Wine Road area, this well-established restaurant specialises in roast meats and fresh trout. In summer, the outdoor tables offer photogenic views over the vines combing the surrounding hills. You can also ask to taste the wines in the stone cellar below. **€€€**

Maribor

Mak Osojnikova 20, https://restavracija-mak.si. Dining at *Mak* is a unique experience. There is no menu, but the chef-owner will prepare you a selection of exquisite fusion dishes; just decide if you want a small, medium or large selection. This award-winning restaurant is popular so it's best to book well in advance. **€€€€**

Ptuj

Gostilna Amadeus Prešernova 36, www.amadeus-ptuj.si. Excellent *gostilna* (tavern) with a typically hearty menu, with both meat and fish dishes well represented – think steak and pepper sauce with dumplings, or trout with pumpkin oil, sour-cream potatoes and seasonal vegetables. **€€**

Gostilna Ribič Dravska 9, https://pan-restavracija.si. *Ribič* serves freshwater fish specialities like *ribje brodet* (fish stew) and *postrv* (trout). Throughout the summer, guests dine on an open-air terrace that looks over the river. **€€€**

Southeast

Čatež

Gostilna ob sotočju budič Zagrebška cesta 9, tel: 04-189 38 58. Longstanding eatery offering a good selection of Slovenian meat and fish dishes with house specialities, including marinated pork fillet and veal medallions. Be sure to try the locally produced Cviček wine. It also offers wine tasting in a nearby vineyard cottage by appointment. Lunch and dinner Mon–Sat. **€€€**

Mokrice

Mokrice Castle Hotel Restaurant Rajec 4, https://mokrice-castle.com/si/restavracija. This exclusive restaurant occupies one of the corner turrets of the *Mokrice Castle Hotel*. The menu features beautifully presented hearty Slovenian dishes, including first-class game and freshwater fish, plus an excellent wine list. **€€€€**

Novo mesto

Gostilna Vovko Ratež 48, https://gostilna-vovko.si. This excellent family haunt prepares Slovenian and French dishes using seasonal local ingredients; also, an extensive selection of good Slovenian wines and home-baked cakes. Attentive service. Tues–Sun. **€€**

Gostišče Loka Zupančičevo sprehajališče 2, www.gostisce-loka.si. The pick of the town's restaurants, both for its breezy waterside location – close to the Šmihelski Bridge – and fresh, Mediterranean-influenced food, such as risotto with prawns and courgettes. **€€€**

Situla Dilančeva ulica 1 www.situla.si. The surprisingly sleek-looking restaurant in this hostel is just the job for a lunchtime *malica*, which could be, for example, grilled cheese or vegetable soup followed by fried chicken with buttered carrots; wash it down with a glass of Cviček from the cellar. **€**

Otočec

Šeruga Sela pri Ratežu, www.seruga.si. This popular family-run agrotourism centre, spread across a complex of traditional farm buildings, lies 4km (2.5 miles) from Otočec Castle. The menu includes rabbit, trout, rural dishes like *štruklji* (dumplings) and *potica* (cake rolls filled with walnuts or poppy seeds), plus the family's home-made Cviček wine. **€€**

Travel essentials

Practical information

Accessible travel

Slovenia is a generally accessible country, which has gone to considerable effort to make tourism as easy as possible for people with disabilities. Ljubljana in particular is leading the way in accessible travel, with the organisation Ljubljana by Wheelchair (www.ljubljanabywheelchair.com) offering a wealth of information to travellers with reduced mobility, including an app that guides users to accessible locations.

Larger hotels across the country offer disabled-friendly rooms and facilities, and many tourist attractions have made adaptations to improve accessibility: for example, the country's top sight, Lake Bled, offers a paved promenade around a stretch of the lake's perimeter, and there are accessible viewpoints.

That being said, some activities – such as the route through the Vintgar Gorge – remain unsuitable for wheelchair-users.

Accommodation

Hotels. Since independence, many hotels that were formerly aimed at the package-tourism market have been upgraded to provide luxurious extras, such as spas and wellness centres. Several small, family-run boutiques have also entered the market. Hotels are graded by the Slovenian Tourist Board: one- and two-star establishments are rather basic; three-stars are comfortable and offer decent service; and four- and five-star hotels are plush and have a range of extra amenities. The most upmarket options are found in the popular resorts of Portorož on the coast and Bled on the edge of Triglav National Park. There are also a couple of high-class, atmospheric castles offering overnight stays at Otočec and Mokrice.

Note that prices shoot up during high season (July–Aug along the coast, and Christmas and New Year in the ski resorts), and that many hotels offer better rates for stays of more than three days.

Private accommodation. In the highly touristed areas, such as the coast, Bled and Bohinj, private accommodation is reasonably priced and of a high standard, ranging from rooms with shared bathrooms to self-catering apartments. Some but not all of the local Tourist Information Centres (TICs) can help you find private accommodation; if a TIC cannot help, try local travel agencies or searching online.

Tourist farms. To gain real insight into rural life in Slovenia, stay at a *turistična kmetija* (agrotourism centre). Ideal for families with children, a stay on a working farm offers direct contact with nature. Most are set in peaceful, unspoilt countryside, and provide authentic home cooking made from local seasonal produce. For further information visit www.slovenia.info.

I'd like a single/double room with a bath/with a shower. **Rad(a) bi enoposteljno/dvoposteljno sobo s kopalno kadjo/s prho.** *rat (raada) bi enopohstelno/dvopohstelno sobo s kopaalno kadyoh/s perrho*

What's the rate per night? **Koliko stane na noč?** *kohliko staane na nohch*

Airports

Ljubljana international airport (www.lju-airport.si) is 23km (14 miles) from the city. From Monday to Friday there is a half-hourly bus service to the centre; at weekends this is reduced to hourly; the last departure from the airport is around 9pm. The journey takes 45 minutes, and tickets can be purchased on the bus, though it is cheaper to buy from ticket machines before boarding. There is also an airport shuttle service run by GoOpti (www.goopti.com). Taxis can be found by turning left out of the arrivals hall: the expected fares are listed online at www.lju-airport.si/en/transport/taxi.

Although Ljubljana is Slovenia's only international airport currently operating scheduled flights, other options include **Trieste** airport in Italy, particularly for the coast, or **Graz** and **Klagenfurt** in Austria.

What bus do I take for the town centre? **Kateri avtobus pelje v center mesta?** *katehri awtobus pehlye oo tsenterr mehsta*

How much is the fare to ...? **Koliko stane do ...?** *kohliko staane do*

Apps

Slovenia has a number of taxi apps, including the fairly universal Uber, as well as Bolt. More local options include **Wizi**, which covers Slovenia, Croatia and North Macedonia. If you're self-driving, you'll need to pay for parking: the **EasyPark** app is, true to its name, easy to use and covers the entire country. When exploring Ljubljana, **Urbana** offers a quick and easy way to pay for public transport, while **Nexto** provides audio-guide tours of the city. Visit www.visitljubljana.com/en/visitors/travel-information/useful-mobile-apps for more suggestions.

Bicycle hire

Cycling is popular in sporty, ecologically minded Slovenia. Ljubljana has a self-service bike-hire scheme with sixty docking stations (www.bicikelj.si), and the Ljubljana Tourist Information Centre (TIC) has bicycles for hire. In Ljubljana and Maribor many locals travel on two wheels, and the city centres have cycle lanes. Bickes are available to rent in any part of the country where you would conceivably want to ride one, most notably in Triglav National Park, where several agencies also organise cycling tours.

Budgeting for your trip

Although reasonably cheap by Western standards, prices in Slovenia are far higher than those in former Eastern Bloc countries such as the Czech Republic and Hungary.

Accommodation. A standard double room with en-suite bathroom and breakfast in a five-star hotel costs around €180 a night, while prices for a double in a three-star range from €60 to €80.

Meals. A three-course meal for two with a bottle of wine in a decent restaurant will set you back around €50. A set-menu lunch (*dnevno kosilo*) in a no-frills *gostilna* (tavern) costs around €12 per person.

Drinks. A bottle of local beer costs around €2.50 in a down-to-earth *gostilna*, and a glass of decent wine in a *vinoteke* (wine bar) €3.50.

Entertainment. A cinema or local chamber concert ticket is around €6, and a full orchestral event is €5–35. Nightclub entry in Ljubljana starts around €5.

Public transport. Trains and buses are inexpensive. City bus fares are slightly over €1 (in Ljubljana a single journey fare is €1.30). Taxi and minibus transfers are around €1 per km.

Car hire. A week's car hire costs upwards of €200, depending on the model and the type of insurance. Petrol is around €1.3 a litre.

Camping

Slovenia has around fifty small, well-equipped campsites. Most are along the coast and in the mountains, and are open May to September. Among those with the best reputation are *Zlatorog* by Lake Bohinj (www.camp-bohinj.si) and *Camping Bled* by Lake Bled (www.sava-hotels-resorts.com/sl/sava-hoteli-bled/kampiranje/kamping-bled). *Ljubljana Resort* (https://ljubljanaresort.com) is 4km (2.5 miles) north of the city centre in Ježica on the banks of the River Sava.

Two campsites cater for naturists: *Camp Smlednik* (www.dm-camp smlednik.si) by Lake Zbilje, 20km (13 miles) north of Ljubljana on the way to Kranj, and *Banovci Spa* (www.terme-banovci.si) in Veržej in the northeast of the country.

Pitching a tent outside organised campsites is not permitted. For further information visit www.slovenia.info/en/plan-your-trip/where-to-stay.

Car hire

International and local car-hire companies operate from Ljubljana Airport and in all the main towns and resorts. Some companies allow one-way rentals to Croatia and Bosnia. To hire a car, you must be 21 or over and hold a valid driving licence.

I'd like to hire a car. **Rad(a) bi najel(a) avto.** *rat (raada) bi nayehw aawto*

I'd like it for a day/a week. **Za en dan/teden.** *za en daan/tehden*

What's the charge per day/week? **Koliko stane na dan/teden?** *kohliko staane na daan/tehden*

Climate

Slovenia has three distinct climatic regions. The mountains have an Alpine climate with warm summers and cold winters with heavy snow; the coast has a Mediterranean climate with hot, sunny summers and mild winters; and the inland region has a continental climate with hot, dry summers and icy winters. Generally, the best periods to visit are May to June or September to October, when you can expect dry, warm weather, ideal for outdoor sports such as hiking and mountain biking. Try to avoid July and August, when temperatures can rise above 30°C (86°F) and tourist destinations are horribly busy, especially on the coast. In the ski season (Dec–March) temperatures can drop as low as –20°C (–4°F) in the mountains. Average temperatures in Ljubljana are:

	J	F	M	A	M	J	J	A	S	O	N	D
Max °C	2	5	10	15	20	24	27	26	22	15	8	4
Min °C	–4	–4	0	4	9	12	14	14	11	6	2	–1
Max °F	36	41	50	59	68	75	81	79	72	59	46	39
Min °F	25	25	32	39	48	54	57	57	52	43	36	30

Crime and safety

Slovenia is safe by any Western European standards. Nonetheless, visitors should take the usual precautions of keeping valuables in a safe place. To report a crime, call the police, tel: **113**.

I want to report a theft. **Prijavil(a) bi krajo.** *priyaaviw (priyaavila) bi kraayo*
Call the police. **Pokličite policijo.** *pokleechite politseeyo*
Stop thief! **Ustavite tatu!** *ustaavite tatoo*
Help! **Na pomoč!** *na pomohch*

Driving

Rules and regulations. Slovenes drive on the right-hand side of the road.

The speed limits are 50kmh (31mph) in residential areas, 90kmh (56mph) on local roads, 100kmh (63mph) on highways, and 130kmh (81mph) on motorways. The police are notoriously tough on those caught speeding (fines are heavy) or drink-driving (0.5g of alcohol per kg of blood is the limit). If you are caught using a mobile phone without a hands-free device while driving, you also risk a stiff fine. Remember that seatbelts must be worn in both the front and the back of the car, and children under 12 are not allowed to sit in the front. Headlights must be switched on *at all times*, even during the day.

Roads. These vary from the slick new motorways to mountain roads, some of which are closed in winter, notably the Vršič Pass. The motorway network is being extended and upgraded. Motorways are subject to toll charges. It is generally cheaper to buy a weekly or monthly vignette (*vinjeta*), available at the borders and at most large petrol stations. This must be displayed when travelling on motorways. There is also a toll for the Karavanke Tunnel (between Slovenia and Austria). Many car-hire companies will automatically include tolls in the price of your booking.

The Automobile Association of Slovenia (tel: 1987; www.amzs.si) provides a 24hr rescue service.

cona za pešce pedestrian zone
delo na cesti road works
enosmerna ulica one way
izvoz exit (motorway)
nevarnost danger
obvoz detour
parkirni proctor parking zone

Electricity

The standard electric current is 220V, 50Hz. Plugs have two round pins. Visitors from the UK and the US will need an adaptor to be able to use electrical appliances.

Embassies and consulates

Embassies and consulates based in Ljubljana:

Australian Consulate Železna 14, tel: 01-234 86 75; https://dfat.gov.au/about-us/our-locations/missions/australian-consulate-in-ljubljana-slovenia.

Canadian Consulate Linhartova 49a, tel: 01-252 44 44; www.international.gc.ca/country-pays/slovenia-slovenie/ljubljana.aspx.

Irish Embassy Poljanski nasip 6, tel: 01-300 89 70; www.ireland.ie/en/slovenia/ljubljana.

New Zealand Honorary Consulate Vodnikova 126, tel: 03-171 55 00.

UK Embassy Trg Republike 3/IV, tel: 01-200 39 10; www.gov.uk/world/organisations/british-embassy-ljubljana.

US Embassy Prešernova 31, tel: 01-200 55 00; https://si.usembassy.gov.

embassy **veleposlaništvo** *veleposlaanishtvo*

Emergencies

Police **113**

Fire Brigade **112**

Ambulance **112**

There's been an accident. **Zgodila se je nesreča.** *zgodeela se ye nesrehcha*

Call a doctor/an ambulance quickly. **Hitro pokličite zdravnika/rešilni avto.** *heetro pokleechite zdrawneeka/resheelni aawto*

Getting there

By air. National carriers offering regular flights to Ljubljana include Air France, LOT, Air Serbia, Lufthansa and Turkish Airlines. British Airways flies to Ljubljana seasonally.

Low-cost carrier easyJet (www.easyjet.com) offers frequent flights from London Gatwick and Manchester to Ljubljana. Ryanair (www.ryanair.com) flies from London Stansted to Trieste in Italy, from where Slovenia can be reached by car – or, if you have a fair bit of patience, by bus or train. Travellers from outside Europe will most likely need to take a connecting flight via London, Paris or Dubai.

By rail. Direct trains run to Slovenia from Italy, Austria, Hungary, Croatia, Serbia and Germany. There are speedy Eurocity services to Ljubljana from Zagreb (journey time 2hr 15min), Venice (4hr), Vienna (4hr 10min) and Munich (6hr 20min).

Eurail one-country passes for Slovenia (www.raileurope.com) are relatively inexpensive, but while the rail network is good, it is limited in where it goes and buses are often a better option.

For national and international information, contact Ljubljana train station: Kolodvorska 11; https://potniski.sz.si.

By bus. Buses run to Slovenia from all its neighbouring countries. If you are departing from the UK, FlixBus (www.flixbus.co.uk) operates a bus service from London Victoria to Ljubljana (journey time approx 30hr) with a change in Munich, Germany.

For national and international bus information, contact Ljubljana bus station: Trg Osvobodilne fronte 4, 1000 Ljubljana; www.ap-ljubljana.si.

By car. There are motorways leading into Slovenia from neighbouring Italy, Austria, Hungary and Croatia. Foreign vehicles from outside the EU require an International Green Card to enter Slovenia, which can be purchased at the border.

Guides and tours

In the capital, Ljubljana Tourist Information Centre (Adamič-Lundrovo nabrežje 2, near Tromostovje, tel: 01-306 12 15; www.visitljubljana.com) offers various tours of Ljubljana, including walking tours of the old town, the historical city centre and Ljubljana Castle, as well as more specialised offerings such as food-focused visits to the market and a cycling tour led by "three moustachioed men". Special rates are available for groups.

The Ljubljana TIC also offers guided tours of Ljubljana by arrangement, and can help arrange excursions outside Ljubljana – such as to the Postojna Caves, Bled, Alpine scenery or vineyards.

In other towns of historical interest, enqu re at the local Tourist Information Centre (TIC) for guided tours.

Note that attractions such as the Lipica Stud Farm, Škocjan Caves and Postojna Cave can be visited only as part of scheduled guided tours.

Is there an English-speaking guide? **Ali kakšen vodnik govori angleško?** *aali kakshen vodneek govoree anglehshko*

Health and medical care

There are no specific health risks in Slovenia, and the water is safe to drink throughout the country. As in much of Central Europe, if you get flu-like symptoms after a tick bite, see a doctor immediately because of the risk of encephalitis.

Members of EU countries are entitled to free emergency medical treatment providing they have a European Health Insurance Card (EHIC) when they travel, which can be obtained at post offices or online at www.ehic.org.uk. For British travellers, a Global Hea th Insurance Card (GHIC) is required, though an existing EHIC can be used up until its expiry date, at which point a GHIC must be obtained (www.nhs.uk/using-the-nhs/healthcare-abroad/apply-for-a-free-uk-global-health-insurance-card-ghic). In an emergency, telephone **112** for an ambulance.

24-hour pharmacies in major towns

Ljubljana Lekarna Ljubljana, Njegoševa cesta 6; www.lekarnaljubljana.si/poslovalnice/lekarna-pri-polikliniki.

Maribor Lekarne Maribor, Ljubljanska 9; www.mb-lekarne.si.

Kranj Lekarna Kranj, Bleiweisova 8; www.gorenjske-lekarne.si/enote-gorenjske-lekarne/lekarna-kranj.

Novo mesto Lekarna Brežice, Kandijska 1; www.lekarna-brezice.si.

Language

Slovenian is a South Slavic language written in Latin script. Most young people speak good English, plus either Italian or German. Older people are more likely to speak Italian as a second language along the coast, and German as a second language in the northeast. Note that on the coast, many places have two names, both Slovenian and Italian, which can be confusing: for example, Koper is also known as Capodistria, and Piran as Pirano.

Pronunciation of most letters is roughly like that in English. However, 'c' is pronounced as 'ts', 'j' as 'y', and in certain words 'v' as if it were 'u'. Accented characters are 'č' as 'ch', 'š' as 'sh', and 'ž', something like the 'ge' in 'orange'.

yes **ja** *ya*
no **ne** *ne*
please **prosim** *prohsim*
thank you **hvala** *hvaala*
good morning **dobro jutro** *dobro yootro*
good afternoon **dober dan** *dohber daan*
good evening **dober večer** *dohber vechehr*
goodbye **na svidenje** *na sveedenye*
excuse me/sorry **oprostite** *oprosteete*
Where? **Kje/Kam?** *kyeh/kaam*
When? **Kdaj?** *kdaay*
How long? **Kako dolgo?** *kakoh dowgo*
How far? **Kako daleč?** *kakoh daalech*
left **levo** *lehvo*
right **desno** *dehsno*
open **odprt** *odperrt*
closed **zaprt** *zaperrt*
old **star** *staar*
new **nov** *now*
early **zgoden** *zgohden*
late **pozen** *pozen*

LGBTQ+ travellers

Slovenia is certainly the most tolerant of the former Yugoslav countries towards LGBTQ+ communities, though it remains less open to public displays of affection than Western Europe. Same-sex sexual activity has been legal since 1977, and the country legalised same-sex marriage in 2022, following a ruling from the Constitutional Court, and in doing so became the first former communist country to do so. The capital held its first Pride – Ljubljana Pride (www.ljubljanapride.org) – in 2001, which has since become an annual one-week event, and there are other regular LGBTQ+ events, including the yearly Pink Week event in May. Note that there remains some intolerance: attendees of Ljubljana's Pride event in 2023 were threatened with homophobic and transphobic verbal and physical abuse. Consult websites such as www.travelgay.com, https://ljubljana.gaycities.com and https://theglobetrotterguys.com for the most up-to-date information for LGBTQ+ travellers in Slovenia.

Money

The Slovenian Tolar (SIT), introduced at independence in 1991, was replaced by the euro (€) in 2007.

Visitors can change foreign currency in banks, post offices and some of the larger hotels. Most banks, even in small provincial towns, have ATMs, and the larger hotels, restaurants and shops accept credit cards.

I want to change some dollars/pounds. **Zamenjal(a) bi nekaj dolarjev/funtov.** *zamehnyaw (zamehnyala) bi nehkay dohlaryerw/foontow*

What's the exchange rate? **Kakšen je menjalni tečaj?** *kaakshen ye menyaalni techaay*

Opening times

Banks. Mon–Fri 9am–5pm, Sat 8am–noon.

Shops. Mon–Fri 8am–7pm, Sat 8am–1pm. Shops selling essential goods are allowed to open on Sundays and public holidays, but Sunday trading has been opposed by the Trade Union of Workers in Trade.

Markets. Most larger towns stage an open-air fruit-and-vegetable market Mon–Sat 7am–2pm.

Museums. The larger museums are generally open Tues–Sun 10am–6pm during summer, with reduced hours in winter. Some of the smaller museums are shut completely through winter.

Petrol stations. Mon–Sat 7am–8pm; major stations open 24 hours.

Police

The police (*policija*) are generally helpful and friendly, though you're unlikely to need much interaction with them.

Tickets issued by police for motoring offences are payable at banks and post offices.

Where's the lost property office/police station? **Kje je urad za najdene predmete/policijska postaja?** *kyeh ye uraat za naaydene predmehte politseeyska postaaya*

My wallet/handbag/passport has been stolen. **Ukradli so mi denarnico/torbico/potni list.** *ukraadli so mi denaarnitso tohrbitso potni leest*

Public holidays

1–2 Jan New Year holidays *novo leto*

8 Feb Slovenian Cultural Holiday *slovenski kulturni praznik*

27 April Resistance Day *dan upora proti okupatorju*

1–2 May Labour Day holidays *praznik dela*

25 June Slovenia Day *dan državnosti*

15 Aug Assumption Day *veliki šmaren (Marijino vnebovzetje)*

31 Oct Reformation Day *dan reformacije*

1 Nov All Saints' Day *dan spomina na mrtve*

25 Dec Christmas Day *božič*

26 Dec Independence Day *dan samostojnosti*
Movable dates:
Easter *velika noč*
Easter Monday *velikonočni ponedeljek*

Telephones

The country code for Slovenia is 386. When calling from outside Slovenia, the first 0 in the area code is dropped. When dialling within Slovenia, the area code is dialled in full unless you are making the call from within that area. City area telephone codes are: 1 (Ljubljana), 2 (Maribor), 4 (Kranj), 5 (Portorož), 7 (Novo mesto).

There are three Slovenian mobile phone networks (Telekom Slovenije, A1 and Telemach). SIM cards and phones are readily available from phone retailers in larger towns, and at Ljubljana Airport on arrival. E-SIMs such as Saily can offer the easiest way to get connected.

For citizens of 31 European Economic Area countries, roaming charges for temporary mobile phone roaming were abolished in mid-2017 – some fair-use policies are still in place, though. Check with your provider what roaming your package allows.

Time zones

Slovenia is one hour ahead of GMT and adopts daylight-saving time in summer.

New York	London	**Ljubljana**	Jo'burg	Sydney	Auckland
6am	11am	**noon**	noon	8pm	10pm

Tipping

If you have enjoyed your meal and thought the service was good, it is usual to leave a tip of around ten percent in restaurants. However, tipping in general is not the custom in Slovenia, though of course appreciated for good service.

Toilets

There are few public toilets other than those found in train and bus stations, where it is usual to pay a small sum. Otherwise, you can always duck inside a café or bar to use their amenities, though in this case it is polite either to ask first, or to buy a quick drink. Generally, toilets, like everything else in Slovenia, are remarkably clean.

Where are the toilets? **Kje je stranišče?** *kyeh ye straneeshche*

Tourist information

The **Slovenian Tourist Board** runs a useful website at www.slovenia.info. There is a Slovenian Tourist Information Centre (TIC) in Ljubljana at Adamič-Lundrovo nabrežje 2, just opposite the Tromostovje bridge, tel: 01-306 12 15. There are also small TICs in the train station and at the airport.

Most other cities and towns and even some villages have their own TIC. Some are listed below:

Northwest

Bled: Cesta svobode 10, tel: 04-574 11 22; www.bled.si.
Bohinj: Ribčev Laz 48, tel: 04-574 60 10; https://tdbohinj.si.
Kranjska Gora: Kolodvorska 1c, tel: 04-580 94 43; www.kranjska-gora.si.
Škofja Loka: Cankarjev trg 17, tel: 04-517 06 00; www.visitskofjaloka.si.

Southwest

Koper: Titov trg 3, tel: 05-148 59 99; https://visitkoper.si.
Piran: Tartinijev trg 2, tel: 05-673 44 40; www.portoroz.si.
Postojna Cave: Trg padlih borcev 5, tel: 04-012 23 18; www.visit-postojna.si.

Northeast

Celje: Glavni trg 17, tel: 03-428 79 36; www.visitcelje.eu.
Maribor: Partizanska 6a, tel: 02-234 66 11; www.visitmaribor.si.
Ptuj: Mestni trg 4, tel: 02-779 60 11; https://visitptuj.eu.

Southeast

Novo mesto: Glavni trg 11, tel: 07-393 92 63; www.visitnovomesto.si.

Transport

It is easy to get around Slovenia on public transport. Most places are within two hours of Ljubljana, so there is no overnight travel involved.

How much is the fare to ...? **Koliko stane vozovnica do ...?**
kohliko staane vozownitsa do
I'd like a ticket to ... please. **Vozovnico do ... prosim.**
vozownitso do prohsim
single (one-way) **enosmerno** *enosmehrno*
return (round trip) **povratno** *povraatno*

Buses. Buses are cheap and efficient, and the network is more extensive than the railways, which is why locals generally prefer buses to trains. In fact, you can reach almost anywhere in the country by bus, though some journeys may involve several changes.
Ljubljana bus station, www.ap-ljubljana.si.
Maribor bus station, www.marprom.si.
Koper bus station, tel: 05-662 51 05.
Trains. Trains are cheap and comfortable, though due to the mountainous nature of the country the railways are less far-reaching than the bus network. The fastest and most frequent city services run from Ljubljana to Maribor, and Ljubljana to Koper. Consult https://potniski.sz.si for train timetables and information.

Worth a special mention are the old-fashioned **steam trains** that operate on several lines during the tourist season, including a steam route through the Soča Valley. For information, visit www.soca-valley.com/en/in-search-of-adventure.
Taxis. Taxis are available in all major towns but are by no means cheap. It's best to try to negotiate a fare before starting a journey. Apps such as Uber tend to offer better rates.

Where can I get a taxi? **Kje lahko dobim taksi?** *kyeh lahkoh dobeem taaksi*
What's the fare to ...? **Koliko stane do ...?** *kohliko staane do*
Take me to this address. **Peljite me na ta naslov.** *pelyeete me na taa naslow*
Please stop here. **Tukaj ustavite, prosim.** *tookay ustaavite prohsim*

Visas and entry requirements

Most foreign visitors need a valid passport to enter Slovenia, though citizens of EU countries and Switzerland can enter the country with just a personal identity card for stays of up to thirty days. For stays of up to ninety days, citizens of EU countries, plus the UK, Norway, Iceland, Liechtenstein, the US, Canada and Australia, can enter Slovenia without visas. However, from late 2026, visa-exempt citizens will need an ETIAS to travel to Slovenia; check https://etias.com for details. South African nationals require visas.

Slovenia is a Schengen Agreement country so there are few controls at the borders with Austria, Croatia and Italy. Visitors from other nations should either visit the website www.gov.si or check with the Slovenian embassy in their own country. **Customs allowances** are the same as for other EU countries. Note that when returning from Slovenia to the UK, goods must be for personal use or a gift (you may not receive any reimbursement).

Websites and internet access

Almost all hotels, restaurants and cafés offer wi-fi access. Here are some useful websites for travel in Slovenia:
www.slovenia.info The Slovenian Tourist Board offers extensive up-to-date coverage of accommodation, transport and activities within the country.
www.sloveniatimes.com An English-language fortnightly newspaper featuring sports, culture, lifestyle and events.
www.gov.si The government's public relations and media website, which files English-language press releases about the country.

Index

MINI
SLOVENIA

First edition 2026

Editor: Joanna Reeves
Authors: Jane Foster and Bill Helmsley
Updater: Owen Morton
Picture Editor: Piotr Kala
Picture Manager: Tom Smyth
Cartography Update: Katie Bennett
Layout: Claire Armstrong
Production Operations Manager: Katie Bennett
Publishing Technology Manager: Rebeka Davies
Head of Publishing: Sarah Clark
Photography Credits: All images Shutterstock and iStock except: Fotolia 66; Neil Buchan-Grant/ Apa Publications 36, 40, 42, 44, 72, 81, 83, 84, 87, 89, 106, 112; Slovenia.info 12BL, 12CR, 14T, 46, 50, 53, 54, 62, 64, 68, 69, 75, 77, 90, 95, 97, 98
Cover Credits: The Pilgrimage Church of the Assumption of Mary, Lake Bled **Shutterstock**

About the author

Owen Morton is based in North Yorkshire, and has written or contributed to numerous Rough Guides, ranging from Shetland to Jordan. When not exploring the world, he entertains himself by writing a blog about 1980s cartoons. His favourite animal is the wonderfully expressive and permanently furious manul, which is native to Central Asia and sadly not Slovenia. Follow him on Instagram at @owenmortonmanul.

Acknowledgements

Owen would like to thank the fantastic team at Rough Guides, particularly editor Jo Reeves, as well as all the hugely welcoming people we met on the road in Slovenia – among many others, the staff at Tržič Gorge were particularly lovely. Thanks also to travelling companion Katherine Morton – exploring Slovenia wouldn't have been such fun without you

Distribution

UK, Ireland and Europe: Apa Publications (UK) Ltd; mail@roughguides.com
United States and Canada: Two Rivers; ips@ingramcontent.com
Australia and New Zealand: Woodslane; info@woodslane.com.au
Worldwide: Apa Publications (UK) Ltd; mail@roughguides.com

Special Sales, Content Licensing and CoPublishing

Rough Guides can be purchased in bulk quantities at discounted prices. We can create special editions, personalized jackets and corporate imprints tailored to your needs.
mail@roughguides.com
roughguides.com

EU Representative

LOGOS EUROPE, 9 rue Nicolas Poussin, 17000, LA ROCHELLE, France; Contact@logoseurope.eu; +33 (0) 667937378

Printed by Finidr in Czech Republic

ISBN: 9781835291948

This book was produced using **Typefi** automated publishing software.

A catalogue record for this book is available from the British Library

Contact us

Every effort has been made to ensure that this publication is accurate, free from safety risks, and provides accurate information. However, changes and errors are inevitable. The publisher is not responsible for any resulting loss, inconvenience, injury or safety concerns arising from the use of this book. If you notice any errors, outdated information, or potential safety risks, please send your comments with the subject line "Rough Guide Mini Slovenia Update" to mail@roughguides.com.